METHODS FOR THE MEASUREMENT OF PSYCHOLOGICAL PERFORMANCE

IBP HANDBOOK No. 10

Methods for the Measurement of Psychological Performance

A HANDBOOK OF RECOMMENDED METHODS
BASED ON AN IUPS/IBP WORKING PARTY

Editor
S. BIESHEUVEL

INTERNATIONAL BIOLOGICAL PROGRAMME

7 MARYLEBONE ROAD, LONDON NW1

BLACKWELL SCIENTIFIC PUBLICATIONS

OXFORD AND EDINBURGH

SBN 632 05980 X

First Published 1969

Printed in Great Britain by
BURGESS AND SON (ABINGDON) LTD.
ABINGDON, BERKSHIRE
and bound by
THE KEMP HALL BINDERY, OXFORD

Contents

Foreword

The series of IBP Handbooks is designed to provide in a handy form the kind of information and guidance which is needed by biologists all over the world so that they can participate effectively in the International Biological Programme. As such the books deal mainly with methodology, especially of environmental biology. This one, however, is concerned not with biology but with psychology. It is a companion to IBP Handbooks Numbers 1 and 9, the three together covering the section of IBP concerned with Human Adaptability; but in Number 10 the field of endeavour is extended from physical and physiological to mental attributes of mankind.

During the early stages of IBP, there was a good deal of discussion whether human adaptability in this context should be so extended. It is one thing to compare and assess the differences in structure and functioning of the human body of races in different parts of the world living under different environmental stresses; it is quite another thing to assess their mental aptitudes, for, if taken out of the scientific context, these can lead to awkward controversy. The purpose of IBP, however, is not only to add to the total of human knowledge, but to organize and co-ordinate that knowledge so that it can be of good service to mankind. Clearly a knowledge of mental and physical attributes, and of their relationships one to another, would be of much greater use than of physical attributes alone. Having decided, therefore, that tests of psychological performance should be included, the HA Section turned to one of the best known exponents in this field, Dr S. Biesheuvel, who was the creator and for many years the director of one of the leading centres in the subject, the Institute for Personnel Research of the Council for Scientific and Industrial Research in South Africa.

Professor J.S. Weiner, the International Convener for Section HA, with the assistance of Dr Biesheuvel, organized a technical meeting of selected specialists covering different aspects of psychological performance testing. This was held in London in September, 1967, through the generosity of

CIBA Foundation. From the wide-ranging discussions at that meeting the form and shape of this handbook emerged.

Such is the origin of this volume, but the subject matter is of such interest and importance, and has been so well sifted and sorted, that it is likely to persist as a reference work long after IBP has ceased to exist in 1972. The Special Committee for the IBP is most grateful to the authors for their contributions and particularly to Dr Biesheuvel for bringing the whole into so comprehensive and yet so concise a form.

E.B. WORTHINGTON

February 1969

Preface

As a result of collaboration between the International Biological Programme and the International Union of Psychological Science, a Working Party on Psychological Performance Measurement was set up to make recommendations on psychological measurements that might be needed or could usefully be obtained in the cause of Human Adaptability Projects.

As Convenor of the Working Party, I attended the Wenner-Gren Symposium on 'The Inter-Relation of Biological and Cultural Adaptation', held at Burg Wartenstein, Austria, in July 1966. This gave an opportunity to determine the needs for psychological measurements that were likely to arise in the Human Adaptability Projects of the IBP and to discuss the best way of meeting these needs with other psychologists at the Symposium.

The Working Party met in London for five days during September 1967 at the Ciba Foundation. I take this opportunity to thank the Ciba Foundation for the Conference and residential facilities that were placed at our disposal at its London Headquarters.

Membership of the Working Party was to be based on extensive theoretical and practical knowledge of cross-cultural testing and its problems in all continents; in the second place on knowledge of specific measurement techniques, but unfortunately some who had accepted membership were eventually unable to attend as the available funds proved insufficient to cover all travelling expenses. Eventually, the following assembled at the London meeting:

Dr S. Biesheuvel	P.O. Box 1099, Johannesburg; Convener and Chairman
Mr C.R. Bell	Environmental Physiology Research Unit, London School of Hygiene & Tropical Medicine
Dr A. Elithorn	Department of Psychological Medicine, Royal Free Hospital, London

Dr J. Ertl	School of Psychology and Education, University of Ottawa, Canada
Professor A. Heron	Institute for Social Research, University of Zambia, Lusaka
Dr D. Jones	External Scientific staff, Medical Research Council, London, and Hon. Clin. Psychologist, Royal Free Hospital and National Hospital for Nervous Diseases, London
Professor G. Jahoda	Department of Psychology, University of Strathclyde, Glasgow
Professor R.S. MacArthur	Department of Educ. Psychology, University of Alberta, Edmonton, Canada
Professor K. Provins	Department of Psychology, School of General Studies, The Australian National University, Canberra, Australia
Mr J. Schepers	National Institute for Personnel Research, Johannesburg, S. Africa
Professor P. Verhaegen	Department of Psychology, University of Louvain, Belgium
Professor P. Vernon	Faculty of Education, University of Calgary, Canada
Professor F. Wickert	Department of Psychology, Michigan State University, East Lansing, Michigan

I thank them as a group for their contributions to our joint proceedings. I must also mention, with appreciation, the assistance I received from Dr S. Irvine, Public Health Service Visiting scholar at the Educational Testing Service, Princeton, Mr. G. Nelson, Head of Department of Neuropsychology, National Institute for Personnel Research, Johannesburg and Mr. I.G. Ord, Chief Psychologist, Public Service Commissioner's Dept., Port Moresby, New Guinea, for their valuable assistance through private discussions and correspondence.

Five sub-committees were set up to prepare drafts on psychophysiological, psychomotor, perceptual and high level mental tests, and on the ancillary individual and group information that would be needed for meaningful interpretation of test data.

The task of preparing, reviewing and collating the drafts of these sub-committees had to be conducted entirely by correspondence. The communication difficulties experienced in this procedure no doubt account for such shortcomings as the handbook may be found to possess. It is the work of many hands, and although an editorial attempt has been made to maintain consistency of presentation throughout, this has not always been possible.

It was originally the intention to include the report in the Handbook on Approved Methods for the Human Adaptability Section. We were, however, unable to meet the target date for going to press. The report also turned out to be considerably longer than had been expected, and it was therefore decided to publish it as a separate monograph in the IBP's Methodology Series.

I am greatly indebted to Professor J.S. Weiner, Convener of the Human Adaptability Section of the IBP for his concern to ensure psychological participation in H.A. projects, for his continued interest in the activities of the Working Party and for obtaining financial support for its procedures. Professor A. Summerfield, Executive Member of the Council of IUPS who has acted in a liaison capacity in London and who provided further financial assistance through IUPS has also been most helpful.

Finally, a word of thanks to my Secretary, Mrs L. Welgemoed, who has efficiently rendered secretarial services to the Working Party, including the typing, re-typing and amending of the many drafts that went to the making of this Handbook.

S. BIESHEUVEL

Johannesburg,
  August 1968

1
Introduction to the Measurement of Human Performance

1 Man's adaptation to environmental change takes place mainly by way of learning and through cultural means. Learning capacity is probably the most important element in human adaptability. But even when adaptation takes place through genetic and physiological means, this may have implications at the psychological level. Both learning capacity and culture formation may be affected. Psychological measurement can be applied both to the immediate and to the long-term effects of stresses that may arise in the course of adaptation to change. It can also throw light on the various ways in which individuals and populations differing in genetic or cultural make-up respond to such stresses. Psychological measurement can never deal directly with genotypical determinants. It can only deal with behaviour as it has developed in the course of growth and interaction with the environment. To what extent the existence of genetic components, their nature and relative importance, can be inferred from phenotypical measurement is still being debated by behavioural scientists.

It follows that in whatever measurements they make, psychologists must always consider the possibility that learning or some aspect of the cultural context within which development took place, has influenced what is being measured. Psychophysiological measures are by no means excluded from this rule.

2 Measurements can therefore best be made within a population which is ethnically and culturally homogeneous, in order that any error or bias exercised by these population characteristics may be held constant. In such homogeneous groups, differences in test performance can be legitimately related to experimental variables. Cross-sectional development studies can trace the growth of abilities and personality characteristics, subject to any particular environmental variations that may occur within the culture or that may be experimentally introduced. Longitudinal studies can give sufficient control of intracultural environmental influences randomly affecting individuals to justify inferences about genotypical components in particular performances.

For such intra-cultural investigations, it is by no means always necessary specifically to construct culturally appropriate tests. Existing tests will be suitable, provided they satisfy the following conditions.

2.1   The test situation and procedure must be so arranged that subjects can be put at ease and will approach the test with interest and reasonable motivation. This may involve changing the procedure laid down in the manual which specifies how the test should be used in the culture for which it was originally devised.

2.2   The test instructions must be given in such a way that the subjects fully understand what is required of them. This may involve translating the instructions into the vernacular, or the use of mime, or demonstrations, or visual aids, or any other method appropriate to the circumstances.

2.3   The method of recording answers, or conveying one's solution must not create problems likely to detract from the quality of the subject's performance. The use of separate answer sheets with coded answers for machine scoring, for example, may create difficulties for subjects who have had little or no schooling.

2.4   The test must discriminate between individuals, i.e. it must give a very wide range of performances from very poor to very good. One would expect test scores to be distributed unimodally. A clump of virtual non-starters at the bottom is a sure indication that the requirements of the test or the nature of the problems posed by it, have not been understood by a sizeable proportion of the sample.

2.5   The test must be reliable. There are two kinds of reliability, namely internal consistency, and consistency between successive performances of the same tests. Internal consistency applies to tests consisting of a series of items. The relationship between the sum of the odd and of the even items, as measured by means of a correlation coefficient, must reach a statistically acceptable standard. In test-retest reliability, which is the more important criterion, there must be a close correlation between the rank-order of performances on a first and subsequent application of the test as a whole, or on successive trials within the same test administration, or on parallel forms of the test.

2.6 The test must be valid, i.e. the individual differences in performance must be related to whatever it is the test purports to measure, again to a statistically acceptable extent. Criteria such as progress in education, examination performance, work performance, success in acquiring or exercising a particular skill, are commonly used.

Validity is, of course, self-evident in direct performance appraisals such as running speed or in threshold measurements such as auditory acuity. In the case of indirect measures, it is desirable to know the factor content of tests. It does not follow, however, that the factor structure of a test is invariate for different cultures. It may measure different attributes under different circumstances and this is an aspect of performance measurement that needs to be separately investigated whenever novel conditions apply.

2.7 Many tests are published with manuals of administration and norms. The latter indicate the standing of individuals within a population for which the test has been standardised. Norms are always relative to the method of administration detailed within the manual, and to the characteristics of the population used for standardisation. If the population with which one is concerned is culturally different from the standardisation group or demands a different test procedure, new norms should be specifically established by re-standardising the test for that culture.

2.8 The problems set by the test must not presume knowledge on the part of the subjects which their culture does not normally provide. This applies for example to the ability to tie shoe laces or to name colours, both items in a well-known developmental test series. Such items have to be replaced with culturally more appropriate ones. Where a test uses this kind of items, however, it is generally necessary to reconstruct it entirely to bring its contents into line with the specific cultural circumstances.

However, provided the subject fully understands what he has to do, the actual content of the tests (such as for example the diagrams used as problems in a reasoning test) or the materials to be manipulated (such as blocks to be arranged in a pattern, or mechanical objects to be sorted) need not in all cases be familiar to the testees. This applies in particular to tests measuring adaptability to new circumstances, where an element of unfamiliarity may be an advantage. On the other hand, if the test sets out to measure how well the subject has learned to deal in the course of his development with the demands made upon him by his environment, i.e. if it contains an element of knowledge and achievement, then clearly the problems must be set in familiar terms.

3   A major measurement problem arises if it is necessary to compare performance in groups differing in culture, i.e. who do not share a common language, cosmology, way of life; who differ markedly in general pattern of child rearing, in modal conformity to social norms, in basic educational background and in exposure to the requirements of our contemporary technological society.

Culture-free tests do not exist, because the behavioural functions measured by tests—other than those at a psychophysiological or sensory level—are all culturally determined. Manner of thinking for example, is strongly influenced by linguistic structure, by semantic categories, and by the way the world is perceived and interpreted. Merely changing a test from a verbal to a pictorial or diagrammatic form, assuming the latter to be equally familiar to different cultures—which is by no means always the case—does not alter the difference in logical or conceptual approach which it will evoke. At the perceptual level we may find that the manner in which the environment is perceived is not only influenced by the visual habits conditioned by the physical features of the childhood environment, but also by the type of conformity that is required within the particular society and the way in which conformity is established and enforced. Even at the level of motor responses, the setting within which the early developmental stages run their course and the opportunities for interaction, are decisive for later development of skills and aptitudes.

To meet the problem of finding a medium through which adaptability can be validly measured cross-culturally, psychometrists have come up with 'culture-fair' tests; by which is meant tests which avoid the more obviously culture-bound features, such as emphasis on speed of performance, pictures presenting objects or situations that lack universality, or even familiarity with the conventions of pictorial representation. The radical problems of the way reality is perceived, the manner in which problems are interpreted, and differences in mode of thought, are unaffected by such modifications. The 'culture-fair' tests merely succeed in reliably measuring individual differences, though what they measure in different cultures may be far from identical. Provided this is realised, and results are used to assess different ways in which cultural groups have adjusted to their particular environmental requirements, performance measurement even by means of tests which have a different cross-cultural significance can still be valuable. When, however, we are concerned with capacity to deal effectively with change, i.e. with adaptability, the problem remains, for there may be no common criterion of effectiveness, and what was genetically given may have been radically affected, in so far as continued potential to meet change is concerned, by cultural circumstances during the developmental period. Only intra-group experiments to determine the limits of modifiability of behaviour at particular development stages, and in response to specific environmental influences, can yield significant information.

4   The methods of performance measurement recommended for use in human adaptability projects must be approached with all the limitations of cross-cultural measurement constantly in mind. By and large, the specialists responsible for recommendations are satisfied that the tests and other measures proposed can be used across a very wide range of cultures, in the sense that they will yield reliable measures of individual differences; but the significance of the measurements obtained will always need to be interpreted in the light of what is known about the tests, the circumstances that affect performance, and the conditions under which the measurements are made. Knowledge about the tests will be given in synoptic form, or references will be included to literature about them.

In Chapter 2, details are given of the ancillary information on habitat, population, sample, individual, and the circumstances under which the measurements were made. Without such information, it will not be possible to compare results from projects carried out by different investigators in different areas. Even within a single, specific project interpretation may be difficult without some of the ancillary information. If special supplementary information is needed for any particular measurement, this will be indicated in the description of the procedure applying to that test.

Recommended tests and other measurements are made under four headings. Chapter 3 deals with psychophysiological measurement, where the cultural problem is least important.

Chapter 4 describes psychomotor performance tests. Here a distinction has been drawn between the skills that people acquire for survival and every-day living and skills which are developed in response to cultural change. In traditional societies the former can best be dealt with by observational or descriptive means, in natural or contrived situations, whereas the latter require measurement by means of tests.

Chapter 5 deals with perceptual responses. References to measures of sensory processes have been included but not described in detail. It is assumed that the standard devices for the measurement of e.g. visual and auditory acuity are sufficiently well-known and generally applicable, though there may well have to be procedural changes to suit specific circumstances. Perception should be studied, not only in order to determine how knowledge is acquired about the environment through the senses, but also on how this knowledge from various sense modalities is integrated, what part is played by non-cognitive factors in this integration, and what we can learn about the state of development and intactness of the central nervous system as mediator of adaptive responses.

Finally, tests for higher mental processes involving reasoning and conceptual thought are discussed in the fourth section. It is at this level that the influence of cultural factors becomes most pronounced, and that the difficulty of recommending measures that can be generally used, even for intra-cultural studies, has proved greatest.

5 Those who need to know more about the cross-cultural application of psychological tests than could be given in this synoptic introduction are referred to the following texts:

BIESHEUVEL S. (1949) Psychological tests and their application to non-European peoples. *The Yearbook of Education.* London, Evans Bros, 87–126.

BIESHEUVEL S. (1952) The study of African ability. *African Studies,* 2, Pt I, pp. 45–58, Pt II, 105–117.

BIESHEUVEL S. (1965) Personnel selection. *Annual Review of Psychology,* **16,** 295–324 (particularly pages 309–316, which deal with personnel selection in developing countries, in which the problem of cross-cultural testing is dealt with and further references are given).

SCHWARZ P.A. (1963) Adapting tests to the cultural setting. *Educ. Psychol. Measmt.,* **23,** 672–86.

VERNON P.E. (1965) Ability factors and environmental influences, *American Psychologist,* **20,** 723–733.

MACARTHUR R.S. (1966) *Mental Abilities in Cross-Cultural Context.* Psychology Colloquium, McGill University, Montreal.

2

Ancillary Information

The interpretation of psychological data will generally require the availability of ancillary information on the samples used for measurements, and on the conditions under which the measurements were obtained. This is particularly important if comparisons are to be made of observations made in different cultures and areas, by different investigators. It is unlikely that conditions will ever be identical, but some allowance can be made for deviation from standard conditions if all relevant circumstances, i.e. those likely to affect the measurements being made, are known. To cover all demographic, geographic, social anthropological and sociological aspects that might be relevant would be an impossible task, and only major features can therefore be taken into account, for which some general prescription can be given. It can be assumed that for the purposes of biological observations and measurements, control data will be available which will supplement psychological control information.

I **FOR THE SAMPLE.** The following ancillary information is needed.

1.1 How the sample was drawn, and the manner in which it represents the parent population. See Wickert F.R. ed. (1967) *Readings in African Psychology from French language Sources*. African Studies Center, East Lansing, Mich. U.S.A., 178–189 and 196–203.

1.2 General description of the parent population (habitat, tribal affiliation, acculturation, brief reference to kinship system and cosmology).

1.3 Conditions under which psychological measurements were performed, whether in the open or in a building, what kind of building, control over extraneous stimuli, availability of visual aids etc.

1.4 By whom the tests were administered, state of training of testers, use of interpreters, degree of rapport achieved, test sophistication of subjects, attitude towards tests and motivation to perform.

1.5 Any special circumstances that could affect test performance (e.g. mothers having to be tested whilst nursing or minding children; seasonal activities in the community that could affect test performances such as pre-occupation with particular rituals).

NOTES ON INFORMATION
RELATING TO SAMPLE

The following notes are provided as a guide to the collection of information for items 1.1 to 1.5.

1.2 HABITAT. Describe physical characteristics, climate (rainfall, temperature range, altitude), seasonal variations.

Biological characteristics (special features of animal and plant life, human population data, particularly numbers and density in significant habitat groupings and source of information).

Economic Foundations provided by habitat (food gathering, hunting, fishing, agriculture, mining, trade, development of economic infra structure, monetary system, rates and levels of economic and technical development. Political aspects of habitat (ethnic policies, land tenure, taxes, outside aid, public order and safety, public information.

ACCULTURATION. State closeness of contact with alien culture, nature of contact, which sectors of population are affected, extent to which institutions are affected (family, church, education, political system); in what way material culture has been affected and how closely; effect on economy, on food habits, on attitudes in so far as ascertainable, on communication system. It may be useful to apply modernity scale (q.v.) to sample.

KINSHIP SYSTEM AND COSMOLOGY. Consult or refer to social anthropological or sociological texts concerning the population when dealing with non-western groups.

1.3   **Conditions under which psychological measurements were performed.**
It is necessary to be precise about the circumstances under which
tests were applied such as time of day, during or after school/work
hours, size of group tested simultaneously, length of test session,
order of tests, number of sessions, precautions taken against
copying, and collaborative attempts to 'beat the tests'.

1.4   **By whom tests were administered.** Full details must be given of age,
sex, race, qualifications and experience of testers, how the tests were
introduced, how rapport was established, in what way subjects
were motivated to take the tests.

NOTE ON QUALIFICATIONS FOR
TEST ADMINISTRATORS

Psychological tests generally require to be administered by trained testers.
The level of training varies according to the nature of the test. In the case of
some tests particularly the perceptual and higher mental tests, the qualifications of testers or of their supervisors are specified by the publishers and
evidence of the adequacy of their qualifications has to be furnished before
test material and manuals are supplied. Research workers who are not
themselves psychologists are strongly urged not to attempt to use any
psychological test without the assistance of properly trained personnel.
Psychophysiological measures, because of their elaborate instrumentation,
require testers experienced in the use of these particular laboratory techniques.
They need not necessarily be psychologists, of course. In the case of electroencephalography, international training standards for recordists have been
laid down. No special training is necessary for the administration of motor
performance tests, apart from the Two-Hand Coordination Test. Physiologists, medical officers and other qualified investigators can use them from
the instructions provided, supplemented where necessary by reference to the
appropriate literature. Because of the many problems presented by cross-
cultural testing, it is advisable that even qualified testers should undergo a
period of training in the use of the particular procedure prescribed for the
population to be tested, if this happens to be different from the one with
which they are familiar.

2   **FOR THE INDIVIDUAL.** An individual record form has been drawn up as follows.

INDIVIDUAL RECORD FORM

Code No..

Surname........................... First name(s) ....

Marital status................ Single .... Married................ Other (specify) ....

1   Sex..................... M......................... F.........................

2   Age..

2.1   (If available) Date of birth: day......................... month......................... year ....

2.2   Claimed age (years)...

2.3   Observer's estimate (if different)   ....

3   **Physical and/or psychological defects/handicaps** ....
....

4   **Family background**

4.1   Schooling of parents/guardians (code highest achieved)

	Father	Mother
No schooling	1	1
Elementary (part or complete)	2	2
Secondary (part or complete)	3	3
Teacher training	4	4
Technical	5	5
College or university (part or complete)	6	6
Other (specify)		

4.2   Occupations of parents/guardians (multiple coding as appropriate)

	Father	Mother
Farming	1	1
Hunting/Fishing	2	2
Craft (indigenous)	3	3
Labouring	4	4
Trading	5	5
Semi-skilled or skilled	6	6
Clerical	7	7
Lower professional administrative or managerial	8	8
Higher professional administrative or managerial	9	9
Other (specify)		

4.3 Siblings

| | Full sibs | | | Half-sibs |
| Age | Education (code as for 4.1) | | Age | Education (code as for 4.1) |

....
....
....

Younger

....
....
....
....

subject

....
....
....

Older

....
....
....
....

N.B. Bracket twins together; mark D for deceased sibs.

4.4 **Description of home setting:** check list, tick or cross as appropriate.
Mud hut, tin shack or similar ....
Brick, stone or wood building ....
Round shape...
Angular shape ....
Western-type furniture ....
Piped water supply ....
Electricity ....
Functional clock ....
Books and/or newspapers ....
Pictures and/or photos ....
Western toys...
Etc..

4.5 Language(s) spoken in home ....
Other(s) spoken by subject...

5 **Occupational history** (adults only)
Present occupation (precise specification of what he does with his hands, etc.)
....
Other occupation(s) in past ....
Note any multiple occupations and/or seasonal changes ....
....

6 Education

6.1 Years of full-time education ....

6.2 Details of schools or other educational institutions attended...
....

6.3 In case of doubt, result of reading and number recognition test;
Reading score.. Number score................................

7 Leisure activities and/or special skills (e.g. athlete, dancer, drummer)
....
....

8 Geographical mobility
Never moved beyond home area (approx. 20 miles)   1
Occasionally moved within rural areas   2
Frequently moved within rural areas   3
Occasionally visited urban areas (approx. 10,000 pop.)   4
Prolonged (over one year) residence in urban areas   5
Other (specify) ....

9 Score on Modernity Scale (male adults only) ....

10 Ethnic, tribal or other sub-group membership (where sample non-homogeneous)
....

11 Specification of interview data collection
Interpreter used: Yes, same sex as testee   1
                  Yes, opposite sex as testee   2
                  No   3
Comments on rapport achieved and response of subject (friendly and helpful, hostile
and suspicious, apparent attempts at concealment, etc.)..
....
....

INFORMATION ON TESTS

In case of any deviation from the procedure specified in appropriate sections, or where information was not sufficiently detailed and some improvisation had to be decided upon, or where test forms were locally printed, or equipment locally manufactured, full information must be given on what was done.

Scoring method must be fully described, if no manual was available, or if for one reason or another there was a deviation from the manual.

If scores are interpreted in terms of norms, reference must be given to these norms and to the population on which they were established.

If local variations of prescribed tests are used, the reliability of these versions must be given, and how it was arrived at.

APPENDIX TO CHAPTER 2
THE MODERNITY SCALE

The exposure of test respondents to the requirements of social organisations of the western type will have a two-fold effect on their test performance. In the first place, through habit formation, deliberate training, formal education, their familiarity with the skills measured by various tests will have increased. In the second place, they will have become attitudinally more adjusted to test situations. They will be less anxious in facing novel tasks and will thus experience less emotional inhibition. They will be more used to working under pressure of time, and will have a better appreciation of the purpose for which they are required to participate. They will accept an element of competitiveness, either with others or with themselves, and will try to turn in an optimum performance. In fact, willingness to participate at all may depend on a sufficient degree of confidence and insight.

Although the personal and social data prescribed as essential ancillary information should give a reasonably good indication of cultural assimilation, an additional quantitative measure will be helpful in the interpretation of test scores, and particularly in their statistical manipulation.

The 'Modernity Scale' is recommended for this purpose. It is adapted from D.H. Smith and A. Inkeles, from whom permission has been obtained for the IBP to utilise the scale in any way useful to the H.A. Programme, subject to suitable acknowledgement being made to the authors in any published reports. A minimum version of their O–M or overall modernity scale has been found appropriate for use in Argentina, Chile, India (Bihar), Pakistan, Israel and Nigeria (Yorubaland). It has also worked well in the Appalachian district of Kentucky, U.S.A., and therefore appears to be suitable for a wide range of different cultures. So far it has only been used for adult males and should not be used for females or male children and youths as the existing version is not appropriate for them.

The content of the scale is as follows.

MINIMUM SCALE OF INDIVIDUAL MODERNITY

1   Have you ever given much thought to, or become highly concerned about some public issue (such as . . .) to the extent that you really wanted to do something about it?
(a) Frequently
(b) Few times
(c) Never

2   If schooling is freely available (if there were no kinds of obstacles) how much schooling (reading and writing) do you think children (the son) of people like yourself should have?

3   Two twelve-year-old boys stopped during their work in the corn (rice) fields. They were trying to think of a way to grow the same amount of corn (rice) with fewer hours of work.
(a) The father of one boy said: 'That is a good thing to think about. Tell me your thoughts about how we should change our ways of growing corn (rice)'.
(b) The father of the other boy said: 'The way to grow corn (rice) is the way we have always done it. Talk about change will waste time but not help.'
Which father said the wiser words?

4   What should most qualify a man to hold high office?
(a) Coming from (right, distinguished or high) family background
(b) Devotion to the old and time-honoured ways
(c) Being the most popular among the people
(d) High education and special knowledge

5   Which is the most important for the future (this country)?
(a) The hard work of the people
(b) Good planning on the part of the government
(c) God's help
(d) Good luck

6   Learned men (scholars, scientists) in the universities are studying such things as what determines whether a baby is a boy or girl and how it is that a seed turns into a plant.
Do you think that these investigations (studies) are;
(a) All very good (beneficial)
(b) All somewhat good (beneficial)
(c) All somewhat harmful
(d) All very harmful

7   (a) Some people say that it is necessary for a man and his wife to limit the number of children to be born so they can take better care of those they do have (already have). (b) Others say that it is wrong for a man and wife purposely (voluntarily) to limit the number of children to be born.
Which of these opinions do you agree with more?

8   Which one of these (following) kinds of news interests you most?
(a) World events (happenings in other countries)
(b) The nation
(c) Your home town (or village)
(d) Sports
(e) Religious (or tribal, cultural) events (ceremonies) or festivals

9   If you were to meet a person who lives in another country a long way off (thousands of kilometers away), could you understand his way of thinking?
(a) Yes
(b) No

10   Do you think a man can truly be good without having any religion at all?
(a) Yes
(b) No

11   Do you belong to any organization (associations, clubs), such as, for example, social clubs, unions, church organizations, political groups, or other groups?
If 'Yes', what are the names of all the organizations you belong to? (Scored for number of organizations).

12   Would you tell me what are the biggest problems you see facing (your country)? Scored for number of problems or words in answer.

13   Where is (in what country is the city of) Washington/Moscow? (Scored correct or incorrect).

14   How often do you (usually) get news and information from newspapers?
(s) Every day
(b) Few times a week
(c) Occasionally (rarely)
(d) Never

INSTRUCTIONS FOR ADMINISTRATION

Use native language interviewers, usually social workers or college students whose social origins are as closely as possible the same as those of the interviewees. With regard to the translation of the questions, follow the usual procedure of back translating until there is agreement among the translators that the questions are conveying reasonably closely the sense of the question as worded in English.

All interviewers then try to stay as closely as possible to the wording developed by the translator team.

INSTRUCTIONS FOR SCORING

Scoring is limited to within-country comparisons. No scoring has yet been devised to permit cross-country comparisons. Even within-country comparisons may be too broad if there are groups within a country that vary widely in cultural outlook.

It is possible to mark the answer of each item response as 'traditional' = 1, or 'modern' = 2. Before final marking, a distribution of recorded answers has to be prepared on each item for each group. Scores below the median (or as close to the median as possible depending on the form of answers for the question) are given a score of 1 and above the median a score of 2. For example, suppose one gets the following distributions of scores (here expressed in percentages of the total to simplify the example) for a four-choice response: choice 1 (low or traditional end of the scale) 40%; choice 2, 25%; choice 3, 20%; and choice 4 (high or modern end), 15%. The break closest to the median is chosen. Here it occurs at 40%. Forty percent is closer to the median (50%) than 40% + 25% = 65%. If the break occurs at a tie point, one simply has to be consistently arbitrary in deciding how to score the marginal response; for one tied item use the break toward the modern end, for the second tied item the break toward the traditional end, etc.

The total modernity score is the sum of the item scores.

The last four items called 'Behaviour-Information Items' in contrast to the 'Pure Attitude Items' (1 to 10 inclusive) may be omitted if time happens to be short.

CODING INSTRUCTIONS AND NOTES

1   Closed coding. The modern end is 'frequently'. In adapting this question to a particular country, it is sometimes advantageous to give examples of public issues, especially if the term 'public issue' is not familiar.

An alternative item asks what would you do about a proposed law which you considered unjust or harmful. This is coded for action versus inaction, action being the modern response (especially collective action).

2   This is an open-ended question, but the interviewer is instructed to probe until the respondent mentions a specific number of years or a level of schooling easily converted into years. This makes direct field coding very simple. The more years of education desired, the more modern the answer.

An alternative item asks what is the best occupation your respondent thinks a person like himself could obtain. This is coded for status level, with high status aspiration coded as modern.

3   Closed coding. The modern answer is to think about new techniques. In the more developed countries (Chile, Argentina, Israel) the following version of 3 was used. 'While some people say that it is useful to exchange (discuss) ideas about new and different ways of doing things, others think that it is not worthwhile since the traditional and familiar ways are best.

Do you feel that thinking about new and different ways (forms) of doing things is:
(a) always useful;
(b) usually useful;
(c) only useful at times;
(d) rarely useful?'

4   Closed coding. The modern end is high education. An alternative item asks whether the basis of social prestige and respect should be education/money/family background, with 'education' considered the modern answer.

5   Closed coding. The two responses scored modern are 'hard work' and 'government planning' given as either the first or the second choice.

An alternative asks whether the respondent prefers work with many/few/or no problems or decisions with the first response being most modern.

6　　　　Closed coding. Answering that 'scientific study is beneficial' is considered modern. In the more developed countries the example 'Why there are earthquakes', may be used instead of 'How it is that a seed turns into a plant'.

7　　　　Closed coding. Modern answer: favours birth control. A more extended response scale should be used when the sample of respondents is known to be quite modern—e.g., ranging from viewing birth control as 'almost always a good idea' down to 'never a proper thing to do'.

8　　　　Closed coding. The more modern answer is considered to be news about world and national events. An alternative asks what two sources of information about world affairs the respondent trusts most, with the modern response being mass media sources as contrasted to personal, non-mass media sources.

9　　　　Closed coding. 'Yes' is coded as the modern answer. The actual name of a distant, very different foreign country may be used (e.g., Japan). Also the response scale may well be extended to include the middle category, 'perhaps'. An alternative item asks whether the respondent enjoys meeting new people or prefers to spend his time with people he already knows. The modern response involves meeting new people.

10　　　Closed coding. 'Yes' is coded as the modern answer. The response scale might be extended to include the middle category, 'perhaps'. An alternative item asks whether a man should give charity to the poor because of generosity or fear (love) of God, with 'generosity' treated as the modern answer.

11　　　To code this item simply count the number of organizations. The modern coding for this item is a higher number. Compulsory unions should, if possible, be omitted from the count. For instance in Israel membership in the Histadrut was omitted. An alternative asks if the respondent had ever written or spoken to a government official about a public issue, the modern response being 'yes' or 'frequently'.

12   The actual name of the respondents' country may be used instead
of the words 'your country'. The most useful coding for this open-
ended item involves a count of the number of 'problems' enumerated
by the respondent. If this proves too difficult in field practice, a
simple count of the number of words in the response will serve
nearly as well. An alternative item is identical in all respects except
that it asks about the problems facing one's town or village. In both
items the modern answer involves more words or themes (problems)
than the more traditional answer.

13   Either may be used here, with preference given to (Moscow).
Semi-closed coding recorded by interviewer. Those who give the
correct identification are scored modern. Alternative items ask who
was John F. Kennedy (or current U.S. president) and who was
Nehru or any other comparable leader of world renown. For more
developed countries more difficult international figures or national
capitals might be substituted.

14   Closed coding. The modern answer is 'every day'. (For more
developed countries one might ask the number of newspapers read
each day or per week). An alternative item asks for frequency of
exposure to the radio, with higher exposure being more modern.

3
Psychophysiological Measurement

1   Psychophysiological measurements are useful in the description of man's state of adaptation to his environment and of the adaptive process itself because such measures throw light on:

1.1   The state of maturity of the central nervous structures and functions, through which, at successive developmental stages, the process of adaptation is achieved.

1.2   The degree of alertness, in neurological terms, with which the individual confronts his adaptive task.

1.3   The degree of stress which he experiences in the process of adaptation.

1.4   The individual differences in the manner in which this stress is experienced and resolved.

1.5   The temporary or permanent damage that may result from stress, or from any other environmental influence that may be brought to bear on the individual during the developmental stage, or after maturity has been reached; and the consequences of this damage for his adaptability and effectiveness in meeting the requirements of his environment.

2   Because the neurological patterns and their somatic correlates differ markedly from individual to individual in response to the same external stimuli and situations, and because these responses may be more or less useful in the process of adaptation, and may have more or less significant consequences for the well being of the individual (e.g. in their relationship to psychosomatic disorders) it is not unlikely that different ethnic and cultural groups will differ in modal patterns and in frequency distribution of patterns. The recording of these patterns is important, not only for the insight which they provide into the nature of the adaptations made under different genetic and environmental circumstances, but also to provide a base line from which the effect of future adaptations to changing circumstances can be determined.

3   It is immaterial that at this stage the precise behavioural significance of particular psychophysiological processes cannot always be specified. The very diversity of response patterns has complicated interpretation, and knowledge in this field is still rapidly increasing as new instrumentation and more effective computer analysis techniques come into use. Heuristic concepts (e.g. 'level of arousal') may be used which are likely to be further clarified as hypotheses to which they give rise are tested. When data have been recorded in sufficient detail they are available for future interpretation in the light of the more complete information on their significance. Meanwhile they have their current value as a descriptive statement.

4   The recording of a number of psychophysiological responses can be done simultaneously, often without the need for additional time or recording equipment. Thus electrical activity of the brain, cardiac, respiratory, vascular and sweating responses can all be recorded simultaneously whilst the subject is in a resting state, or responding to sensory stimuli, or performing a prescribed mental task. The same polygraph can be used to record responses, or they may be transferred to the same tape for future use.

5   A further important aspect of psychophysiological measurement is that the act of measurement as such poses few if any problems in cross-cultural settings. The subject undergoes many of the measurements passively. The problem of the correct interpretation on his part of what is required from him, which is always a complicating factor in the case of other psychological measures, does not arise. Difficulties are occasionally experienced as in obtaining EEG records from infants in certain cultures, where beliefs concerning the fontanelle cause mothers to resist the fixing of electrodes on the baby's head. Apprehension on the part of a subject about undergoing the test procedure can also create artefacts initially; but these extrinsic cultural sources of disturbance can be overcome. Intrinsic cultural influences are of course an entirely different matter, being in themselves phenomena that need to be noted as affecting the adaptive process. Ancillary observations may be necessary to control such influences. Recent research developments suggest a relationship between certain aspects of intelligence test performance and brain potentials which in view of the serious cross-cultural difficulties associated with the measurement of intelligence, may open up more valid methods of measurement.

In the personality domain, the psychosomatic approach also has some advantages, in that the behavioural criteria that we normally employ are closely culture bound. Research now holds out some promise that certain basic aspects of personality, having to do with alertness, flexibility, predisposition to maladjustment, can be measured by neuropsychological means.

6 The often elaborate instrumentation that is needed for psychophysiological measurement is not as serious a deterrent in case of field investigations as it used to be. Provided facilities are available to transfer observations to tape, the further processing and analysis can be carried out at base. Mobile laboratories facilitate field observations, particularly if they are air conditioned and fitted with a power supply. Alternatively it should be possible to use battery-operated recording and stimulating equipment, and a tent or similar collapsible shelter to control the environment within which observations are made to some extent. A station wagon, truck or vehicle of the landrover type will accommodate most of the equipment one may need.

7 The physiological functions about whose behavioural implications our knowledge is most complete, which have some relevance to the

stress phenomena with which we are concerned in the Human
Adaptability Programme, and which are capable of being measured
in the field comprise the following:
electrical activities of the brain, as reflected in the electroencephalogram;
electrical activities of the autonomic nervous system, as measured
through changes in skin potential and resistance;
peripheral vasomotor changes, reflected in the finger plethysmogram;
heart and breathing rhythms, measured by means of cardiotachometry and the pneumogram.

The rationale for observing these functions and the methods of
measurement will be discussed in some detail. Wherever international conventions exist on instrumentation and procedure, reference will be made to these without going into further detail. Well-
established and generally used techniques (such as blood pressure
measurement) will also be assumed to be familiar to the research
worker. Where full details are given, these should serve as a guide
to ensure comparability of results, but alternative methods can of
course be employed, or modifications can be made to suit local
circumstances or to fit in with the available facilities. Provided
complete information is given on all aspects of equipment, procedure
and processing of data that will affect results, comparability need
not be disturbed.

The most up-to-date and comprehensive textbook to be consulted
is: Venables P.H. and Martin I. (1967) *A Manual of Psychophysiological Methods*. North-Holland Publishing Co, Amsterdam.

NOTE In terms of the classification of Field Work Activities, made
in the Guide to Human Adaptability Proposals (H.A. 60), the
psychophysiological measures described would generally come
under the heading of 'B, Additional Activities' or 'C, Specialised
Activities', depending on the nature of the project.

7.1, electroencephalography, might well be considered an A
activity in nutritional or developmental studies.

7.2, skin potential and resistance would always rank as a C activity.
This would also apply to

7.4, cardiotachometry, except in work capacity studies, where it
might rank as B. Ultimately, however, this is a decision that must

be left to the designers of projects, in accordance with their interests and resources.

7.1   **Electroencephalography.** The electroencephalogram (EEG) is a record of the electrical activity of the brain, recorded from the intact scalp.

7.1.1   RATIONALE OF THE EEG. The EEG can be recorded while the patient is in a resting condition, both with eyes closed and open, or is responding to stimuli, or is asleep or under the influence of drugs. EEG variables can be related to specific physiological brain functions and their psychological correlates. From these we can describe EEG parameters and make deductions regarding the maturity of cerebral development; the stability of certain aspects of neural organisation and function; the existence of brain damage, its location and possible nature and causation; the type of organisation peculiar to the individual subject; the effect of cultural factors on brain function.

For the purposes of H.A. projects of the IBP, this information can be used to establish EEG norms, for particular ethnic groups or cultures; to determine the incidence of clinical abnormalities within these groups; to determine changes in the parameters or in the frequency of abnormalities as groups adapt to changing circumstances; to determine the effects of a number of conditions associated with particular environments or ways of life that may adversely affect brain development, such as malnutrition, anoxia and certain tropical diseases. The EEG is also useful in providing a base line for the study of drug effects.

Considerably more information is obtainable from the electrical activity of the brain if use is made of evoked potentials that can be induced to occur in the EEG, for example by means of randomly spaced light flashes or clicks. There are latent periods between the stimulus and the sequence of potentials evoked by it, and recent research has suggested a significant relationship between these latencies and intelligence test performance. In view of the difficulties experienced in obtaining comparable measures of intelligence cross-culturally, this aspect of the EEG should be of particular interest to H.A. projects. At this stage, however, it should be looked upon as primarily of research interest, as the nature of the relationship that has been observed requires further analysis.

By means of the same techniques, it is also possible to analyse potentials evoked in the EEG prior ($\frac{1}{2}$ sec) to some voluntary act on the part of the subject, such as speech.

7.1.2   INSTRUMENTATION

7.1.2.1   *Basic*
Electroencephalograph meeting the specifications of the International Federation of Societies for Electroencephalography and Clinical Neurophysiology (IFSECN).
Stimulator to provide high-intensity blue-white or orange flashes at 1 to 100 flashes per second, with provision for auditory stimulation (clicks) at 1 to 100 per second.

7.1.2.2   *Additional*
(i) Transducers for cardio tachometric data, plethysmogram, pneumogram etc.
(ii) Magnetic tape storage system for off-line analysis: an F.M. tape recorder of high quality, using either 1-inch tape (9 tracks) or $\frac{1}{4}$-inch tape (7 tracks) and ancillary equipment, such as an analogue-digital convertor.

Data may be stored on tape in either analogue or digital form for off-line analysis by general or special purpose computer. Either a large computer (e.g. I.B.M. System 360) or a special purpose device such as the T.M.C. Computer of Average Transients can be used to provide the following: frequency spectra, power-density spectra, cross-correlation, evoked potential detection and peak identification.

7.1.3   TEST PROCEDURE

7.1.3.1   *Clinical electroencephalography.* Electrodes should be placed in accordance with the procedure recommended by the International Federation of Societies for Electroencephalography and Clinical Neurophysiology (IFSECN), i.e. the 10–20 system. The examination should include at least 10 minutes for recording each with anterior-posterior and lateral electrode montages, or the equivalent if more than two montages are employed. Recording on each montage should include eye-opening and eye closure. The standard activation methods of photic stimulation (at one to at least 30 flashes per second) and hyperventilation (three minutes) should be included.

7.1.3.2 *Detailed EEG study.* This should include such variables as: frequency, amplitude, location, persistence, wave-form and responsiveness of dominant and other electrical activity; degree and type of responsiveness to photic and auditory stimulation; degree, type aud persistence of changes produced by hyperventilation; frequency and power-density spectra; cross-correlation between cerebral hemispheres, or between anterior and posterior areas; auto-correlation; latency of evoked responses to flashes and clicks.

7.1.4 DATA ANALYSIS

7.1.4.1 *Clinical evaluation.* The *clinical evaluation* of the record comprises the identification and judgement of the type or types of abnormality present in the 'resting record', during and following hyperventilation and during photic stimulation, with an overall assessment of the EEG and, finally, an interpretation indicating the possible clinical significance of the findings in the light of the case-history. Where the latter is normal, an interpretation should nevertheless be offered, based on the degree of abnormality of the record and type of abnormality, e.g., focal or generalized; episodic or continuous.

7.1.4.2 *Detailed EEG Study.* Electronic methods of data reduction can yield information on all the variables referred to under 7.1.3.2. Computer programmes are available or can be adapted.

7.1.5 ANCILLARY OBSERVATION. It will be useful to record the following ancillary observations, depending on the nature of the investigation that is being carried out: age, sex, racial origin, customary habitat (altitude, temperature range, geographic area etc.), medical history with special reference to fevers, infections, head injuries, headaches, fainting spells; habits relating to drugs, alcohol, smoking; cultural circumstances as specified elsewhere in this manual.

7.1.6   SAMPLING. Sample size will depend on the purpose for which observations are made. To establish cross-cultural norms it will be necessary to randomise within samples stratified according to age, sex, racial origin and such cultural features in respect of which it is desired to exercise control. Numbers within each cell should not be less than 30. For investigations concerning specific effects (e.g. nutrititional, clinical) not less than 50 cases would be necessary.

7.2   Skin resistance

7.2.1   NATURE OF PHENOMENON. When an externally applied current passes through the skin, resistance is encountered which varies according to the activity of sweat glands or possibly according to the pre-secretory activity of sweat gland membranes. Variations correspond to changes in the state of alertness of the subject, which accompany attention to stimuli, both of a cognitive and of an affective nature. A characteristic wave-form is produced which is generally known in psychological literature as the psychogalvanic reflex (PGR) or galvanic skin reflex (GSR). Its significance derives mainly from its relationship to level of arousal, rather than from its association with emotional responses for which it was believed in the past to be a useful indicator. The GSR fairly rapidly disappears when a sensory stimulus (e.g. a click presented through earphones) is presented at regular intervals. It behaves in fact like an investigatory reflex, the response gradually extinguishing itself as the stimulus requires no further attention on the part of the subject. There are, however, considerable individual differences in the rate of extinction which are characteristic and stable for a particular individual. The number of repetitions of the stimulus required to achieve extinction or a predetermined level of diminution in terms of resistance change can be used as a measure of the subject's level of arousal.

In recording the GSR the investigator has the choice of two main techniques: (1) the resistance method described above (the exosomatic technique, showing the Fere phenomenon) and (2) the potential method (the endosomatic technique, showing the Tarchanoff phenomenon or change in skin potential).

The advantages and disadvantages of each of these techniques are discussed in detail by Thompson R.F., Lindsley D.B. and Eason R.G. in Physiological Psychology, chapter 3 in Sidowski J.B. (ed.) (1966) *Experimental Methods and Instrumentation in Psychology*, New York, McGraw-Hill; and by Gormezano I., in Classical Conditioning, chapter 9 in the same volume.

7.2.2   RATIONALE. The measurement of level of arousal is of interest in H.A. projects, mainly from a research point of view, as throwing some light on constitutional differences in people, having some bearing on their personal tempo, mode of responding to environmental stimuli, possibly on vigilance. Differences can be expected to occur in different ethnic groups, but their full significance cannot at this stage be postulated.

7.2.3   INSTRUMENTATION. In order to minimize the effects of polarization, Ag/AgCl electrodes should be used. The data obtained will depend on a number of physical factors such as the type, placement, size and pressure of the electrodes on the skin. In order to render the results of different studies comparable, it is recommended that sponge electrodes with an area of approximately 1 sq. cm. be attached with a rubber band to the palm and dorsal surface of one hand, and a current of 0·2 V passed through them.

If the exosomatic technique is used a D–C EEG amplifier connected through a Wheatstone bridge is required. Valid data can be obtained by the endosomatic method without a bridge of this kind and even with an R–C amplifier, provided the time-constant is at least 1 second.

For further details see *Manual of Psychophysiological Methods*, chapter 2, Skin resistance and skin potential by Venables and Martin, North Holland Publishing Co, Amsterdam and John Wiley and Sons Inc, New York, 1967, in addition to the source cited in 7.3.1.

7.2.4   TEST PROCEDURE. Electrodes are to be fixed on the palm of one hand, and a current of 0·2 V passed through them. The subject should be seated in quiet surroundings. Sound stimuli are to be presented through earphones, which as far as possible should exclude extraneous sound. Stimulation should start after an initial settling period of five minutes, the stimulus interval to be 30 secs. Data can be recorded directly on tape, or on the EEG polygraph.

7.2.5 ANCILLARY OBSERVATIONS. As in the case of EEG observations, though there is no need to take a detailed medical history.

7.2.6 SAMPLING. As in the case of EEG observations.

7.3 **Cardio-vascular and respiratory responses.** Cardiac, vascular and respiratory changes are among the more important somatic components of behaviour, indicative of the level of arousal at which the behaviour occurs, of the extent of affective involvement, the individual's momentary or chronic state of tension or adjustment, and individual differences in respect of stimulability, flexibility or variability. These reactions should prove particularly important in measuring the amount of stress experienced by individuals or groups in transition from one culture to another and the resulting state of basic emotional tension, of significance in relation to effort, work capacity, interpersonal relations and psychosomatic disorders. A means is also provided of distinguishing between the relative stressfulness of particular tasks or situations, according to their difficulty or affective significance. Considerable cultural differences are known to exist with regard to the latter, and the study of overt behaviour does not always disclose the full impact of these differences.

The interrelationship between cardio-vascular and respiratory functions is close and because of interaction effects, measurements must generally be made simultaneously in respect of more than one manifestation, even though one function may be singled out for particular attention.

7.3.1 FINGER PLETHYSMOGRAM. The state of dilatation or constriction of the peripheral bloodvessels can be most conveniently measured by means of changes in the volume of the finger, though an alternative method is to measure the bloodflow in terms of transparency of finger or ear lobe, a beam of light and photo-electric cell being used for this purpose.

7.3.1.1 *Rationale of the finger plethysmogram.* Mental activity is accompanied by peripheral vaso-constriction or dilation, initiated respectively by the sympathetic and parasympathetic functions of the autonomic nervous system. Thus the solving of a simple arithmetic problem is accompanied by slight vaso-constriction, indicative of a change in the state of arousal of the organism. When arousal also involves emotional responses, sympathetic activity is more pronounced.

Individuals vary considerably in vascular tonus. In some the sympathetic function chronically predominates, in others the parasympathetic. The central tendency of the distribution of ratios between sympathetic and parasympathetic involvement observed in the individuals comprising a particular population can be defined as the autonomic balance for that population, a state intermediate between vaso-constriction and vaso-dilation. The degree of deviation or autonomic imbalance *chronically* displayed by an individual with reference to a normal group mean represents the basic emotional tension of that person. It is represented in the finger plethysmogram by the pulse volume or amplitude, measured as the bloodflow between the base and the apex of the systolic stroke.

Deviations towards either sympathetic or parasympathetic predominance are by no means always indications of impaired adjustment, the individual's predominant balance being merely typical of his particular personality organisation. Basic emotional tension is, however, indicative of the *type* of maladjustment to which the individual would be predisposed, parasympathetic predominance tending towards dissociative (hysterical) reaction, sympathetic predominance towards anxiety reactions.

Phasic deviations from the basic emotional tension, in response to any stimulus causing excitation of the autonomic system, are indicated by changes in *finger volume;* reduction in volume resulting from peripheral vaso-constriction is brought about by sympathetic predominance; an increase in volume, resulting from vasodilation, is brought about by parasympathetic predominance. The *rate of change* indicates the relative ease with which either system becomes predominant over the other. Rate of change in volume thus gives a measure of vaso-motor lability, the ease with which an individual's autonomic balance is disturbed. The labile-stabile dichotomy has been shown to be related to emotional stability. The greater the vasomotor lability, the greater the probability of, or potentiality for emotional instability.

7.3.1.2 *Instrumentation.* A cylindrically shaped capsule or cuff, made of glass or plastic material, open at one end, closed at the other except for a narrow outlet, is made to fit the index finger. The open end should have a flange of about 3 mm, which should lie exactly in the finger groove at the level of the distal interphalangeal joint. The width of the cuff should be such that the finger does not touch the inside, and the fit should not be so tight as to interfere with venous drainage from the finger tip. A series of cuffs ranging in size from 12–20 mm in steps of $\frac{1}{2}$ mm or 1 mm should be available. To obtain an airtight seal between the flange and the finger, silicone stopcock grease is recommended as a sealing medium. The orifice of the cuff is connected by means of low density polythene tubing of 3 or 4 mm internal diameter to an electronic transducer, to convert volume changes into electric signals which after amplification produce a tracing through a polygraph. A suitable complete system manufactured by the Grass Instrument Company consists of a PT5 volumetric low-pressure transducer with 5 Pl pre-amplifier and Model 5 Polygraph. A two-way tap should be inserted in the tubing for calibration purposes and in order that the cuff may remain in contact with the atmosphere when it is fitted. An air leak must be permitted when recording the rapid volume changes corresponding to peripheral pulse beats; but an air tight system is needed for the much slower finger volume changes.

7.3.1.3 *Test procedure.* Because peripheral vascular conditions are particularly affected by temperature, observations must be made in a room which can be kept at constant temperature, preferably within a range of 24°–27° C, with variations limited to 1° either way. There should be no draughts and relative humidity should be between 50% and 60%. Because vascular changes readily occur in response to extraneous stimuli that attract attention, it is desirable to carry out the test in a relatively noiseless darkened room in which the subject can be screened from the recording apparatus. It is evident that field observations will be impracticable unless a mobile air-conditioned laboratory is available.

The subject should be comfortably seated in a semi-reclining position. To ensure maximum vaso-dilation, and also to eliminate initial variations in hand temperature, both hands are kept for 10 minutes in a warm water bath, kept at 40° by means of a thermostat. This period is also useful to induce a state of relaxation in the subject and to explain that all he will be required to do is to answer a few simple questions. Examples of these questions can be given. The position of the arm, on a padded rest, should be abducted about 5° from the subject's side, elbow at 90°, forearm midway between supination and pronation, hand placed round padded 5 cm peg, wrist slightly dorsiflexed, finger semi-flexed and approximately at the level of the heart. Because changes in blood pressure and in breathing can alter peripheral circulation, records of blood pressure and respiration must be obtained concurrently with the finger plethysmogram. For the recording of respiration, see para 7.5.2. For blood pressure recording, a sphygmomanometer cuff, fixed to the right arm, is kept inflated to 40 mm Hg. Pressure changes are converted through a transducer to electrical signals and recorded with the plethysmogram by the polygraph.

Four different plethysmographic records are obtained from each subject:

(a) With the subject completely relaxed and before any task is given. The left hand remains immersed in the warm water bath to retain reflex vaso-dilation.

(b) With the left hand transferred to a cold water bath, kept as near as possible to 18″ C. This would show the amount of vaso-dilation that occurred in response to the previous immersion in warm water. The smaller the decrease in finger volume after change-over, the less the dilatation produced by the warm water, and therefore the greater the amount of chronic vaso-constriction and basic emotional tension.

(c) The subject inhales deeply and holds his breath for as long as possible. The purpose of this procedure is as in (b).

(d) The subject is given a few very simple arithmetic operations, like 8×3, 12×5. Thereafter he is asked to give the answers to some more difficult items like 19×13, $8\frac{1}{2} \times 14\frac{1}{2}$, $17\frac{1}{2} \div 4\frac{1}{2}$. Depending on the purpose and circumstances of the experiment, he could also be asked some questions with possible affective significance, such as 'Is there any person whom you hate?'; 'Think of some situation that would embarrass you.'

After the conclusion of the recording, the volume of the experimental finger is measured in cc by immersion in a measuring glass up to a predetermined point which must be constant for all subjects.

7.3.1.4 *Data analysis*

(a) Rate of change in finger volume (R) for mental tasks is expressed as the change per second per 1000 cm³ finger volume, from the formula

$$R = \frac{1000\,D}{FU.T}, \text{ where:}$$

D = total reflex deviation of finger volume with a task.
T = duration of reflex volume deviation in seconds.
FU = volume of experimental finger.

If instead of the *rate* of reflex finger volume change, the total change i.e. the change in cm³ per 1000 cm³ finger volume (V) is wanted, the formula becomes

$$V = \frac{1000\,D}{FU}.$$

The magnitude of R or V can best be expressed as the mean of the values obtained for the separate tasks.

(b) The above two formulae also apply for the calculation of R_w, and R_b rate of reflex finger volume change with the cold water test and with deep breathing respectively, and for the calculation of V_w and V_b total reflex finger volume change in cold water and with deep breathing respectively.

(c) Pulse volume (P) is read directly in cm³ from the calibrated plethysmograph trace, as the distance between the base and apex of the systolic stroke. The median volume of 6–10 pulse beats should be calculated for P. Values of P should be obtained before the performance of tasks, during the performance of tasks and during the cold water and breathing tests (P, P_t, P_w, P_b).

(d) The variation in pulse volume during the performance of tasks (PV) is obtained from the formula

$$PV = \frac{1000}{P} \, (P{-}P_t),$$

which also applies to the variation with the cold water and deep breathing tests.

(e) A low P value is indicative of sympathetic predominance, and provides less scope for further vaso-constriction in response to task performance than in the case of an equally labile subject recording a higher P value. These two subjects would therefore obtain different R scores. To correct for this error, the effect of P should be statistically removed from R scores. This can be done for each subject by means of the formula:

$R^1 = R - B \, (P - \overline{P})$ in which

R is the subject's rate of finger volume change during task performance or cold water test,

P is the subject's absolute pulse volume before task performance.

$\overline{P}$ is the mean P score in a random sample of subjects.

B is the regression coefficient of R on P in the sample.

R^1 is the derived (corrected) R score.

7.3.1.5 *Ancillary observations.* Mention has already been made of the need to have simultaneous recordings of blood pressure and respiratory changes, to facilitate the interpretation of vasomotor changes (see 7.3.3). Another aspect of cardiac function that might well be included with the plethysmogram is sinus arrythmia, the fluctuations in heart rhythm which normally occur when man is at rest, but which are suppressed or which even out during performance of an intellectual task. (See 7.3.2.)

To facilitate interpretation of the psychosomatic data, it would also be useful to have a psychological measure of emotional stability; but this presents difficulties that cannot at present be overcome in the domain of cross-cultural measurement. The usual adjustment inventories have some validity for distinguishing between adjusted and neurotic persons in specific western cultures; but the manifestations of maladjustment vary from culture to culture and such scales are therefore not generally applicable. In any investigation which is concerned with stress and its effects it would, however, be worth while to take a life history, noting family relations, past illnesses, current state of health, effectiveness of adjustment to the social environment, in terms of criteria relevant to the culture within which the individual was brought up and the new or transitional culture to which he is in the process of adjusting.

7.3.1.6   *Sampling*. Sampling will depend on the purpose of the investigation. If the state of autonomic balance of a particular population is required, it would be as well to use a large random sample of some few hundred cases. For other purposes, samples stratified according to factors that are likely to have a bearing on the state of adjustment one is interested in, such as sex, age, degree of acculturation, should be drawn. Numbers within each ultimate cell should not be less than 30.

7.4   **Cardiotachometry.** It would be inappropriate to attempt to give full details of the measurement of cardiac functions other than those to which reference has already been made in relation to the plethysmogram. If measurements are required because the particular functions are of psychosomatic significance, specialised physiological texts should be consulted. This subject is generally too complex to to be dealt with in synoptic form. Reference should also be made to Venables and Martin's *Manual of Psychophysiological Methods* (op. cit.).

7.4.1   SINUS ARRYTHMIA. A brief reference must, however, be made to the momentary fluctuations in the cardiac cycle known as sinus arrythmia.

7.4.1.1   *Rationale*. These fluctuations diminish and eventually disappear with progressive increase of the amount of information that has to be processed by the central nervous system (as in a binary choice task, in which signals are presented at an increasing rate). However, the degree of suppression is also dependent on individual reserve cerebral capacity, which in turn may depend on the extent to which the individual's information-processing capacity is pre-empted by pre-occupation or emotional reactions. Sinus arrythmia can completely disappear without any increase in pulse rate, and as acceleration of the pulse is a frequent correlate of emotional responses, this characteristic might enable one to distinguish between states of arousal with and without emotional components. The simultaneous recording of vasomotor reactions by means of the finger plethysmogram and sinus arrythmia should prove particularly useful, as the same rest periods and tasks can be used for both. Both are indicative of changes in state of arousal, but the former is more susceptible to emotional reactions and together they should provide a clearer picture of the nature of the stress which the individual is experiencing at a given moment.

7.4.1.2 *Instrumentation, procedure and data analysis.* There are many ways in which the sequence of heartbeats can be recorded. The sequential pattern is much more important than the mean number of strokes per unit of time. The most reliable measure of heart rate response is the 'peak to valley difference', which is the difference between the highest and lowest rate occurring within 20 inter-heart beat intervals. A non-integrating cardio-tachometer which measures the time between two successive peaks of the heart cycle and converts this into a tracing of stroke frequency per minute, is the most useful recording device. When a line is drawn by inspection through the mean frequency and a number of tolerance lines at distances of 3, 6 and 9 strokes above and below this mean, the number of crossings per minute of any one of these lines can be treated as an arrythmia score. A comparison can then be made between arrythmia score during rest, not less than (3 min) and during experimental conditions. By feeding data from the tachometer into a computer as well as into a polygraph, a statistically more precise calculation can be made.

7.4.2 RESPIRATORY ARRYTHMIA

7.4.2.1 *Rationale.* The relationship between variations in respiration and heart rate is complex and mediated through a number of reflex factors. Sinus arrythmia could be changed, if not suppressed by deliberate or other changes in breathing frequency or amplitude.

For control purposes, the breathing pattern must therefore be concurrently recorded.

7.4.2.2   *Instrumentation, procedure and data analysis.* A number of methods are available to obtain a record of frequency and depth of respiration.

A pneumatic strain gauge tied around the chest, consisting of a rubber cylinder about 1 inch in diameter and 12 inches long, sealed at one end and at the other end open to a thin tube leading to transducer and polygraph, is one of the simplest ways.

Another method uses an electrical strain gauge consisting of a 1–5 mm rubber tube sealed at both ends and with metal terminals. The tube is filled with a fluid substance with easily measurable electrical resistance (mercury, aqueous colloidal graphite). Tied with a nylon cord around the chest, the tube stretches and recoils with breathing, and changes the distance and thus the resistance between the terminals. A Wheatstone bridge circuit and polygraph will provide a graphic record of the respiratory sequence. A thermistor measuring temperature changes in nose and mouth with in- and exhalation has an advantage over the strain gauge method in that it is unaffected by chest movements unrelated to respiration; but it may be less comfortable, in having to be fixed to the nostril.

Respiratory cycle time is measured from the onset of one inspiration to the onset of the next. Depth of respiration is given by the amplitude of the respiratory curve. The percentage inhalation time is the ratio of inspiration to the duration of the respiratory cycle (inspiration plus expiration).

4

Psychomotor Performance Measurement

Three deceptively simple questions form a background to the tests described in this section. These questions are: (1) what is the nature of human skills? (2) how are human skills acquired? and (3) to what extent are human skills biologically and culturally determined? To provide, in reply to these questions, answers which would be other than preliminary and tentative would require an infinitely greater research effort than is implied in the testing programmes described here. However, the five test procedures which have been selected can provide some information which, at least, is relevant to these three questions, even though this information, by itself, cannot provide the complex answers that the questions demand.

Although in the last half century, considerable data have been collected by educational, industrial and experimental psychologists and by neurologists, anatomists and ergonomists, all working from their particular orientations to the topic of psychomotor, or more specifically perceptual-motor skills, there are still ample opportunities to pursue information in areas relatively unexplored.

It would probably be true to say that the evolution of man's manual skills has been one of the most important aspects of his evolutionary history. The rapid acceleration of technological progress over the last century or so in some societies stands in sharp contrast to the relatively unsophisticated, perhaps primitive, level of technology in other societies. Yet even within any society, at whatever level of technological development it may be, considerable variety may be seen in the psychomotor skills possessed by its members.

The assessment of perceptual-motor performance within the context of the International Biological Programme can, therefore, afford a useful contribution to that knowledge of man's development in various societies and of his variety of achievement within any one society which is necessary to the formulation of parts of the answers to the three questions which form a background to the test procedures offered here. They relate to the assessment of (1) uni-manual hand-grip strength; (2) finger dexterity; (3) two-hand co-ordination; (4) throwing ability; and (5) balancing skill.

Before describing these tests, reference must be made to what might be called a 'descriptive', as distinct from a measurement technique which has its place in the study of psychomotor performance, namely, the cinematographic record.

The observation of movement skills developed in response to the demands made and the interests aroused by the natural environment provides a good starting point for later systematic studies in which the situations are contrived, or skills themselves are analysed or subjected to greater control. The movements one has in mind are those involved in gathering food such as climbing trees to pick fruit, spearing fish, stalking game; in locomotion, such as paddling a canoe, balancing a load on the head whilst walking, in handicrafts or arts such as weaving, making pottery, or playing musical instruments; and in games or rituals such as dancing, wrestling and throwing. Both the form and pattern of the movements, and the manner of their development are of interest. The cine-camera is the only effective means of providing a record which apart from its descriptive value, also lends itself to detailed analysis of movement sequences.

For an example of the use of this technique, reference should be made to Gajdusek's developmental studies in New Guinea (E. Richard Sorenson and D. Carleton Gajdusek. *The Study of Child Behavior and Development in Primitive Cultures,* Supplement to *Pediatrics,* The Journal of the American Academy of Pediatrics, Vol. 37, January 1966, No. 1, Part II).

NOTE. No attempt will be made to classify the following tests under the heading of A, B, or C activities. Classification will depend entirely on the nature and needs of particular projects. If, however, the need arises to use motor performance tests in any H.A. project, it is suggested that tests 1, 2, 4 and 5 should always be applied together, whereas 3 is more likely to be suitable for specialised C projects.

I   THE MEASUREMENT OF HAND-GRIP STRENGTH

1.1   Introduction

1.1.1   RATIONALE. Muscle strength is an important component in the development of any motor skill and may be especially relevant in studies of motor development during physical growth. Hand-grip strength is particularly important in the investigation of physical activities involving manual performance. A good relationship has been shown to exist between measures of hand-grip strength and measures of the strength of other muscle groups (see for example Roberts, Provins & Morton, 1959).

Considerable data are already available on hand-grip strength and some relevant studies are listed below, although the same apparatus and procedure may not have been used in each case. Particular caution should be exercised in making comparison from one study to another where a non-adjustable dynamometer has been used. In general the test should be administered in a controlled environment. However the test would be suitable for use in abnormal environmental conditions and in both cases details of air temperature, humidity, air movement and the subject's clothing should be recorded on the data proforma.

1.1.2   OBSERVATIONS TO BE MADE. It is suggested that observations of hand-grip strength be made with each hand alone for each subject and for subjects of both sexes from the age of approximately five years.

1.1.3   SAMPLING. In sampling populations on hand-grip strength performance, it is suggested that the measure be taken at one-yearly or two-yearly intervals until physical growth is completed. In adults hand-grip strength should be measured at intervals of approximately ten years. Subjects of both sexes should be studied, and observations should be made both longitudinally and cross-sectionally if possible. For each particular variable being controlled, at least 25 subjects should be studied. However, it is recognised that in practice it will probably be a case of testing the subjects who have been asked to participate in other studies. In these circumstances, of course, the age and sex details of the subject should be noted on the hand-grip performance data sheet.

1.2   TECHNIQUE (INSTRUCTIONS TO OBSERVER)

1.2.1   Test procedure
The adjustable hand-grip dynamometer to be used in these studies is the simple mechanical adjustable type, available from C.H.

Stoelting Co., 424 North Homan Avenue, Chicago 24, Ill., U.S.A.

The test should always record performance achieved with bare hands.

(a) Adjust the dynamometer to the appropriate setting for the size of the subject's hand by placing the instrument in the subject's hand and zeroing the dial pointer as described in the pamphlet obtainable with the recommended dynamometer.

(b) Demonstrate to the subject how the dynamometer is gripped and show how gripping causes the pointer to move around the dial face. Demonstrate this to the subject with each hand in turn.

(c) Give the adjusted dynamometer to the subject, allowing the subject to choose which hand he uses first.

(d) The subject is asked to gradually increase his grip on the dynamometer until the pointer has moved around the dial face as far as he can make it go.

(e) The subject returns the dynamometer to the observer who records the maximum reading and whether the subject has used his right or left hand. The subject's attention is drawn to the performance achieved. The dynamometer pointer is returned to zero and the instrument placed in the subject's other hand.

(f) The subject is asked to repeat the procedure until three readings have been taken on each side in alternate order.

A specimen proforma for recording the data gathered by the procedure described above is given in the Appendix to the section on psychomotor performance measurement.

1.2.2   ANCILLARY INFORMATION

Note should be made on the data sheet of the following information about the subject: (a) sex, (b) age, (c) height, (d) weight, (e) hand size, (f) finger length, (g) dry bulb, (h) wet bulb, (i) air vent, (j) clothing.

In addition, a description should be recorded of any aspects of the individual's previous experience which is considered may have influenced his performance on the hand-grip test. This should include such factors as manual occupation and other activities involving frequent or prolonged hand usage.

1.3   References

BOWERS L.E. (1961) Investigation of the relationships of hand size and lower arm girths to hand-grip strength as measured by selected hand dynamometers. *Res. Quart.* **32**, 308–314.

ROBERTS D.F., PROVINS K.A. and MORTON R.J. (1959) Arm strength and body dimensions. *Human Biol.* **31**, 334–343.

2   FINGER DEXTERITY

2.1   Introduction

2.1.1   RATIONALE. Finger dexterity is seen in the performance of fine manipulative tasks (usually against time) and is known to be influenced by a number of environmental factors such as ambient temperature, air movement and rain (or wet fingers, etc.), as well as by the extent of previous training or practice. Performance on any test of finger dexterity is affected by practice on that particular task so that the usefulness of the achievement level on one test in predicting performance on another manipulative task is strictly limited (see, for example, Seashore, 1951).

Familiarity with materials being used in a test of dexterity is important and almost any apparatus task suffers from this difficulty in cross-cultural testing. Metal objects are also likely to impose special problems in situations of extreme heat or cold. A very large variety of tasks has been used for different purposes and the one recommended here has been selected primarily for its simplicity of equipment and suitability for use in extreme climates (see Gaydos, 1958; Gaydos & Dusek, 1958).

2.1.2   INSTRUMENTATION. The equipment required is a set of approximately 80 wooden blocks (1 in. cubes) with $^3/_{16}$ in. holes drilled through the centre of each side. A blunted metal needle $2\frac{1}{2}$ in. long and $^1/_{16}$ in. diameter with a length of string attached to the eye provides the stringing or threading device. A stop-watch is required to time the performance. (If nearest metrical equivalents are used, actual dimensions must be stated).

2.1.3   OBSERVATIONS TO BE MADE AND SAMPLING
It is suggested that observations of finger dexterity using this test
may be made on subjects of both sexes from the age of approximately 5 years. If possible, they should be made both longitudinally
and cross-sectionally, and for each variable being controlled (e.g.
age, sex or climate), at least 25 subjects should be studied.

2.2   Technique (instructions to observer)

2.2.1   TEST PROCEDURE
(a) The subject performs this test with his bare hands but without
being able to see what he is doing (a blindfold or screen eliminating
visual cues enhances the value of sensory information from the
fingers). A modified and more exacting version of this test for use
with full visual control may be employed by using $\frac{1}{2}$ in. cubes of
wood with $^1/_8$ in. holes in each face and a needle $^1/_{16}$ in. diameter but
$1\frac{1}{2}$ in. long instead of the dimensions given in (a).
(b) A tray of randomly heaped cubes should be placed just below
elbow height in front of the subject who is asked to take the threading needle in his preferred hand.
(c) The subject is asked to thread as many wooden cubes as he
can within a 30 second period, but he is instructed to pick up only
one block at a time with his non-preferred hand and to thread this
on the needle before taking another cube.
(d) At the end of the first 30 second period, the experimenter
should count and record the number of blocks threaded and
whether the subject held the stringing needle in his right or left hand.
(e) The blocks should be returned to the tray and the subject
told the time taken.
(f) The needle is then given back to the subject who is asked to
repeat the performance with the threader in his other hand. This
procedure is repeated until three performances have been recorded
with the threading device in each hand alternately.
A specimen pro-forma for recording the data gathered by the
procedure described above is included in the Appendix.

2.2.2   ANCILLARY INFORMATION. Note should be made on the data
sheet of the following information about the subject: (a) sex, (b)

age, (c) occupation, (d) environmental temperature, (e) humidity, (f) air movement, (g) clothing worn, (h) previous practice on this or similar tasks.

2.3 References

GAYDOS H.F. (1958) Effect on complex manual performance of cooling the body while maintaining the hands at normal temperatures. *J. appl. Physiol.* **12,** 373–376.

GAYDOS H.F. & DUSEK E.R. (1958) Effects of localized hand cooling versus total body cooling on manual performance. *J. appl. Physiol.* **12,** 377–380.

SEASHORE R.H. (1951) Work and motor performance. In: *Handbook of Experimental Psychology,* Ed. S.S. Stevens. Wiley, New York.

3 TWO-HAND CO-ORDINATION

3.1 Introduction

3.1.1 RATIONALE. Most sensory motor tests, whether they involve the use of one limb or more, tend to be highly specific. An exception, which appears to have wider 'general-purpose' value, is the type of two-hand co-ordination test introduced by Moede (1935). In principle, it reproduces the movements of a compound slide on a lathe, and was originally intended as a specific test for the selection of candidates most likely to succeed as lathe operators. However, it has also shown validity for many other tasks requiring fine, co-ordinated movements, such as flying an aeroplane.

As the subject's performance, in addition to being timed is recorded graphically, both a measure of quantity and quality is obtainable. With 'smoothness' of line as the quality criterion, it is possible to distinguish good co-ordination, where the subject has simultaneously integrated the rotation of both handles, from poor co-ordination where he has led with one handle and then followed up with the other.

3.1.2 INSTRUMENTATION. The recommended model has been constructed by the Central Workshops of the South African Council for Scientific and Industrial Research. A full-scale set of constructional drawings may be obtained from The National Institute for Personnel Research, (N.I.P.R.) P.O. Box 10319, Johannesburg, South Africa.

The apparatus consists essentially of a metal platform carrying a printed track on a piece of stout paper under a stationary pencil (a 3H or 5H kept very sharp). By means of two lead-screws, each having sixteen threads per inch, terminating in handles and set at right angles to each other, the subject can cause the platform to travel in two directions, laterally and fore-and-aft, and so make the paper track describe any desired locus under the point of the pencil.

The pencil is gripped by a set-screw at the end of a weighted arm which can hinge out of the way for fitting the paper tracks to the platform and removing them. The platform is provided with spring-loaded clips at the ends to hold the paper in place.

The whole metal structure of the apparatus is mounted to the wooden base-board on a system of 'three-point' suspension so that atmospheric change is less likely to distort the alignment of the bearings and guide bars. For comparative purposes, it is essential that a standard track should be used, printed on strong, evenly finished paper. For each trial, a new sheet must be used. A specimen copy is given in the appendix. The tracing pencil must be kept sharp and an ample supply should be available. A stop-watch is needed to time performance.

3.2   Technique (instructions to observer)

3.2.1   TEST PROCEDURE.

(a) The subject performs the task with his bare hands and uses his two hands simultaneously.

(b) Instructions to the subject are as follows:

'This is a test of your hand co-ordination. This handle moves the paper from left to right (demonstrate to the subject by winding the handle in each direction and allow the subject to imitate the observer's demonstration). This handle moves the paper backwards and forwards (demonstrate to the subject by winding the handle in each direction and allow the subject to imitate the observer's demonstration).

'If you use the two handles together you can move the paper in any direction (demonstrate to the subject by winding both handles simultaneously in one direction and then winding both handles simultaneously in the opposite direction and allow the subject to imitate the observer's demonstration).

'I want you, by using both handles together, to guide the pencil down here, round the circle in the direction of the arrow and back to this cross which I am drawing here (observer inserts pencil cross, freehand, at arrow base).

'In this test you are scored according to the time you take to go round and every time you touch a line it is counted as an error.

'You have five attempts. In each attempt you must work as quickly as you possibly can, making as few mistakes as possible. Your first trial is a practice one. *Remember, it is important that you work as quickly as you possibly can, and try to complete the task more quickly each time you attempt it'*.

(c) Scoring procedures for (i) speed, (ii) errors and (iii) quality are as follows:

(i) *Speed:* This is the average time taken (in seconds) to complete the task in the subject's last four trials. In assessing a total time score, five seconds are added to the actual time taken on each trial for every crossing of the red-boundary line.

(ii) *Errors:* Although for most purposes it will not be found very useful to treat the number of crossings of the red boundary line as an independent score because the occurrence of such errors is very sparse with many subjects, it is suggested that it may be worthwhile to make such observations here.

(iii) *Quality:* This score is a subjective numerical assessment of the quality of the line as an indication of smoothness and co-ordination of movement. A scale of 0 to 5 (unco-ordinated to smooth co-ordination) is used for each trial. The 'quality' score is the total assessment for the five trials. This method of assessing the quality of performance is based on experience, careful observation, and frequent reference to selections of assessed specimens which may be obtained on enquiry from the National Institute for Personnel Research at the address given above.

(d) Samples of two-hand co-ordination performance should be obtained from subjects of both sexes from the age of ten or so years with at least twenty-five subjects of any given characteristic providing data in any one culture.

A scoring sheet for recording performance data is included in the Appendix.

3.2.2   ANCILLARY INFORMATION. Note should be made on the data sheet of the following information about the subject: (a) sex, (b) age, (c) occupation (with particular description of its manipulative content), (d) environmental temperature, (e) humidity, (f) air movement, (g) clothing worn, (h) previous practice on this or similar tasks—
(a) Occupationally.
(b) Non-occupationally.

3.3   **Reference**
MOEDE W. (1935) *Arbeitstechnik*. Stuttgart, Ferdinand Enka Verlag.

4   THROWING SKILL AND HANDEDNESS

4.1   Introduction

4.1.1   RATIONALE. Throwing is a motor skill developed at an early age and with a variety of objects. In hunting communities it may form a vital part of the process of stalking and killing animals for food while in some groups it may form an integral part of a number of different occupations. It is also a common feature of a wide variety of games and sports.

As with finger dexterity, performance on any test of throwing ability is dependent on the extent of previous practice on that task or in similar activities. Familiarity with the type of object to be thrown is also likely to be important, and the hand used (i.e. whether right or left) is likely to be a major variable to be controlled as there is evidence to suggest that throwing may be the best single measure of a person's handedness (see, for example, Humphrey, 1951).

It would be desirable to measure both throwing for accuracy and throwing for distance but there are many difficulties in employing either type of test cross-culturally. The former raises problems of apparatus while the latter presents difficulties of convenience. However, as questions of convenience may be considered to be less important than those associated with complexities of apparatus, tests of throwing for distance are recommended here.

4.1.2   INSTRUMENTATION. The equipment required is a surveyor's tape for marking out the ground and measuring distances of throws, six baseballs of approved match specifications (weight 5 ozs. circumference not less than 9 in. or more than $9\frac{1}{4}$ in.), and six marker stakes. The specified balls may be obtained from Universal Sports Corporation, 9 East 40th Street, New York, New York 10016, U.S.A.

4.1.3   OBSERVATIONS TO BE MADE AND SAMPLING
It is suggested that observation of throwing skill and handedness using this test may be made on subjects of both sexes from the age of approximately five years. If possible they should be made both longitudinally and cross-sectionally, and for each variable being controlled (e.g. age or sex) at least 25 subjects should be studied.

4.2   Technique (instructions to observer)

4.2.1   TEST PROCEDURE A
(a) The test must be administered out of doors where sufficient clear space is available.

(b) Two parallel lines, each 2 metres long and placed 2 metres apart, provide the starting zone. At right angles to these lines, and projecting through their centres in the direction in which the ball is thrown, a third line is marked on the ground to indicate the direction in which the subject should aim his throws. For convenience this third line may be extended and marked off at suitable intervals to facilitate the calculation of distances thrown.

(c) The subject is led to his starting zone and asked to take a baseball in his preferred hand and to throw it overarm as far as possible in the direction indicated by the aiming line. He is told to keep within the parallel lines whilst throwing but he is allowed to take one or two steps (as appropriate) during the throw providing he does not overstep the area marked out.

(d) The place where the ball first touches the ground after it has been thrown is then marked with a marker stake which indicates the hand used and whether it was the first, second or third ball thrown with that hand.

(e) The subject is then given another ball and asked to throw it with his other hand (i.e. the left hand if the first ball was thrown with the right) and the procedure repeated. Six throws should be made altogether—three with each hand being used alternately.

(f) At the end of the six throws, the distance of each marker stake from the intersection of the restraining line and aiming line of the starting zone should be recorded and the subject informed of his results.

4.2.2   TEST PROCEDURE B

If circumstances do not permit the use of baseballs and/or the measurement of throws, a simplified version of this task would be to observe throws of any suitable sized object (or objects such as stones matched for size) and to assess distances thrown with each hand alternately for degree of hand dominance. In this method, a subject should be handed a missile and asked to throw it with his preferred hand as far as possible in a given direction. The location of its fall should be observed and the subject should then be told to try to throw as far or further with the other hand. The location of the fall of the second missile should be observed and a note made on the record sheet as to whether the right or left handed throw was furthest. Ten such pairs of observations should be made for each subject, thus giving ten recordings of the superior hand on the data sheet.

A specimen pro-forma for recording the data gathered by either of the above procedures is attached.

4.2.3   ANCILLARY INFORMATION

Note should be made on the data sheet of the following information about the subject:

(a) sex, (b) age, (c) occupation, (d) environmental temperature, (e) humidity, (f) air movement (direction and speed relative to direction of throws), (g) clothing worn, (h) previous practice on this or similar tasks.

4.3   References

HUMPHREY M.E. (1951) The consistency of hand usage. *Brit. J. Educ. Psych.* **21,** 214–225.

5   BALANCING

5.1   Introduction

5.1.1   RATIONALE. In many respects balance provides a good overall indication of the development of muscle co-ordination. Timing performance on a balancing task, particularly balancing on one leg, is a simple and useful test of muscle co-ordination at a fairly high level, although it must be acknowledged that the personality factors of motivation and persistence are more likely to influence performance here than in most simple motor tests.

5.1.2   INSTRUMENTATION. The only equipment required is a stop-watch to time performance and a flat board large enough for the subject to stand on.

5.1.3   OBSERVATIONS TO BE MADE AND SAMPLING
It is suggested that observations of balancing ability using this test may be made on subjects of both sexes from the age of approximately 5 years. If possible, they should be made both longitudinally and cross-sectionally, and at least 25 subjects should be studied for each variable controlled.

5.2   Technique (instructions to observer)

5.2.1   TEST PROCEDURE
(a) The subject is instructed to remove his footwear, if any, and to stand on the board. He is then told to close his eyes and to stand on one foot with his arms raised sideways so that they are parallel to the floor. The other leg is to be raised with the knee bent so that the thigh is parallel to the floor and the lower leg vertical.
This stance should be demonstrated to the subject.

(b) The leg used for standing should be noted and the time to over-balancing is recorded.

(c) The procedure is repeated with the subject instructed to stand on the other leg.

(d) Record one further trial with each leg in the same order as the previous trials.

A specimen pro-forma for recording the data obtained in this test is included in the Appendix.

5.2.2   ANCILLARY INFORMATION
The following information about the subject should be recorded on the data sheet:

(a) sex, (b) age, (c) occupation, (d) environmental temperature, (e) humidity, (f) air movement, (g) clothing worn—special note should be made of any garments likely to impair performance, (h) previous practice in this or similar tasks.

APPENDIX

PROFORMA RECORD SHEETS FOR PSYCHOMOTOR TESTS

1   Record sheet of hand-grip dynamometer performance

Observer: Name
Address of Base Institute:
Subject's name and/or code number:
Date of observations:
Place of observation:
Environmental conditions: ....° C dry bulb, ...° C wet bulb,
.... cms/sec air movement.
Clothing worn during trials: ....
....

Sex:
Age:
Height:
Weight:
Hand-size:
Finger-length:

GRIPSTRENGTH READINGS: (record hand used in each instance and maximum dial reading, in pounds).

	Hand used (Right or left)	Dial reading (lbs)
1.		
2.		
3.		
4.		
5.		
6.		

BACKGROUND DATA: A description of any aspect of the individual's previous experience which it is considered may have influenced performance on the hand-grip test. This should include such factors as manual occupation and other activities involving frequent or prolonged hand usage:

2   Record sheet of performance, Finger Dexterity Test:

Subject's name and/or code number:
Date of observations:
Observer: Name:
Address of Base Institute:
Place of Observation:
Environmental conditions: ....° dry bulb, ...° C wet bulb, ... cms/sec air movement.
Clothing worn ....
....

Sex:
Age:
Occupation:
Previous practice:

PERFORMANCE READINGS: (record hand used for holding needle in each instance and number of blocks threaded).

	Hand used (Right or left)	Blocks threaded
1.		
2.		
3.		
4.		
5.		
6.		

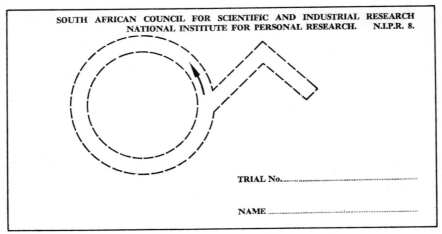

Figure 1. The track shown with a broken line outline is printed in red on the test cards used.

3 Record sheet of performance

TWO-HAND CO-ORDINATOR: (attach subject's performance papers 1–5 to this sheet).

Observer's Name:

Address of Base Institute:

Subject's name and/or code number:

Date of observations:

Place of observations:

Environmental conditions: ....° C dry bulb; ....° C wet bulb; .... cm/sec air movement.

Subject's clothing worn during the trials:..............................

....

Subject's

Sex: .... Age: ....

Occupation: ....

Previous practice: ....

PERFORMANCE READINGS:

	Trial 1	Trial 2	Trial 3	Trial 4	Trial 5
Time taken to complete the track (seconds)					
Number of errors (crossings of red boundary—see Figure 1)					
Error correction (5 sec × number of errors)					
Quality rating (0–5)					

4 Record sheet of performance

THROWING SKILL AND HANDEDNESS TEST
Subject's name and/or code number:
Date of observations:
Observer: Name:
Address of Base Institute:
Place of observation:
Environmental conditions: ....° C dry bulb, ...° C wet bulb; .... cms/sec air movement.

Direction of wind .... (i.e. from N.E.).....
Direction of throws .... (i.e. towards N.W.)
Clothing worn ....
....

Sex:
Age:
Occupation:
Previous practice:

PERFORMANCE READINGS:

Test Procedure A		*Test Procedure B*	
Hand used (Right or left)	Distance thrown (in metres)	Paired Comparison	Superior hand (Right or left)
1.		1.	
2.		2.	
3.		3.	
4.		4.	
5.		5.	
6.		6.	
		7.	
		8.	
		9.	
		10.	

5   Record sheet of Performance

BALANCING TEST
Subject's name and/or code number:
Date of observations:
Observer: Name:
Address of Base Institute:
Place of Observation:
Environmental conditions: ....° C dry bulb, ...° C wet bulb;
.... cms/sec air movement.
Clothing worn:..
....

Sex:
Age:
Occupation:
Previous practice:

PERFORMANCE READINGS:

Trials	Time in seconds	Leg used
1		
2		
3		
4		

5

Perceptual Responses

Perceptual responses range all the way from primary sensory processes, such as absolute and differential thresholds, through perceptual illusions and alternation phenomena to higher cognitive functions such as the perception of space and time. Through the study of perceptual phenomena light can be thrown on the integrative functions of the central nervous system and its intactness, and on the dynamical aspects of the organisation of the personality of man involving the interaction of cognitive and temperamental parameters. The range of phenomena that can be measured is extremely wide, and only a few of these can be discussed for the purposes of the H.A. programme.

Measures will be dealt with under two headings:
1. Primary sensory processes.
2. Adaptive Perceptual integration.

Measures to be discussed under the second of the above headings overlap with tests dealt with in the next section on Higher Mental Processes. The perception of spatial relations is frequently used as a medium for the measurement of mental power because it is relatively free from specific cultural associations, though by no means free from cultural influences in their broadest sense. The emphasis in such tests is, however, on the relational or problem solving aspect, rather than on the perceptual function as such and this distinction determined whether a measure was discussed in this or in the following section.

The tests most likely to be appropriate for major A projects are those concerned with sensory acuity and intersensory transfer, particularly the Rod and Frame Test and the Embedded Figures Test. Perception of Time and Geometric Illusions would come under the heading of special studies. The remainder are all suitable for B Projects, as defined in the Guide to Human Adaptability proposals, though it must be stressed again that the choice must be determined by the particular needs of a project.

▮ PRIMARY SENSORY PROCESSES

1.1 Visual Acuity

1.1.1   EQUIPMENT. Optometric techniques are likely to be more practicable in field investigations than psychological laboratory methods of threshold measurement. Some optometric techniques demand reading ability on the part of the subjects or assume an ability to communicate clearly what is perceived. In any group where literacy is at a low level, use should be made of the Illiterate E Test chart of the American Optical Company.

1.1.2   PROCEDURE
Each subject stands 20 feet away from the chart, which is fixed to a tree so that the midday sun is behind the subject but shines obliquely on to the chart. The subject is shown how to manipulate a cut-out masonite 'E' (14 × 10 cm) into one of four positions, to accord with that of the E pointed out on the chart by the tester. An eye-shade is used to occlude each eye alternately while the uncovered eye is tested, and thereafter the subject is tested binocularly. The subject is familiarized with the procedure by practising on the larger letters, so that it can be noted whether or not he understands instructions. The procedure and scoring method are those of standard visual testing, the Snellen testing procedure for the Letters Chart.

1.1.3   REFERENCE. It is recommended that the following papers be consulted for more detail.
HUMPHRISS D. & WINTER W. (1968) 'An inter-racial study of the acuity of vision'. *Brit. J. Physiol. Optics* (In preparation).

1.2 Auditory acuity. Subjects respond to stimuli by raising the hand when they perceive the signal and until the signal ends. Standard audiometric techniques have been successfully used in the field on groups such as Kalahari Bushmen.

1.2.1   EQUIPMENT AND PROCEDURE. Portable audiometers are readily available, but it is recommended that the following documents be consulted before purchasing an audiometer: IEC publication No. 177 (1965) 'Pure-tone audiometers for general diagnostic purposes'. IEC publication No. 178 (1965) 'Pure-tone screening audiometers'.

It is imperative that audiometers be carefully calibrated before use in audiometric studies. The following publication should be consulted in this regard: ISO recommendation R389 (1964) 'Standard reference zero for the calibration of pure-tone audiometers'.

International Organization for Standardization, Central Secretariat, 1, rue de Varembé 1211, Geneva 20.

If a sound-proof room is not available, the measurements should be taken in the open field. The ambient noise level should preferably not exceed 40 decibels and should be recorded routinely. A well calibrated noise level meter is required for this purpose. The following publications should be consulted in this regard:

IEC publication No. 123 (1961) 'Recommendations for sound-level meters'.

IEC publication No. 179 (1965) 'Precision sound-level meters'.

ISO recommendation R357 (1963)' Expression of the power and intensity levels of sound or noise'.

ISO recommendation R532 (1966) 'Method for calculating loudness level'.

1.2.2   REFERENCES

IEC and ISO publications are obtainable from respectively:
Central Office of International Electro-technical Commission, and International Organization for standardization, Central Secretariat, 1, rue de Varembé 1211, Geneva 20.

DAVIS, HALLOWELL (1947) *Hearing and Deafness: a Guide for the Layman.* Murray Hill Books Inc.

GLORIG, ARAM, ed. (1965) *Audiometry Principles and Practices.* The William and Wilkins Co., Baltimore.

HERON A. & CHOWN S. (1967) *Age and Function,* London, Churchill.

VAN DER SANDT W.A., GLORIG A. & DICKSON R. Survey of acuity of hearing in Kalahari Bushmen. *International Journal of Audiology* (In preparation).

1.3   **Colour blindness.** Several colour blindness tests are available. Some assume an ability to read letters or digits. Plates 18024 in the

Ishihara Colour-Blindness Test have been specially designed for use with illiterates. Subjects are required to trace a winding path between two X's with the aid of a small brush.

The plates are designed for use in a room which is adequately lit by daylight. Direct sunlight or electric light may produce discrepant results because of an alteration in the appearance of the different shades of colour. The plates should be held 75 cm from the subject and should be tilted so that the plane of the paper is at right angles to the line of vision. Each tracing should be completed within ten seconds.

The 24 plates edition (1966) is published by: Kanehara Shuppan Co. Ltd., 31–14, 2-chome Yushima, Bunkyoku, Tokyo, Japan.

1.3.1   REFERENCE
BELCHER S.J. *et al.* (1958) 'Colour Vision Survey'. *Brit. J. Opthalmol.,* **42,** 355–359.

1.4   Tactile discrimination

1.4.1   RATIONALE. Tactile discrimination is particularly important in jobs demanding a high degree of fine manual dexterity. Finger dexterity is interfered with under conditions of extreme cold due to numbness of the fingers. Tests of tactile discrimination can be used to compute indices of numbness which can be used in conjunction with measures of finger dexterity. Numbness indices are also very important in gauging the degree to which individuals have adapted to extremely cold environments.

1.4.2   EQUIPMENT AND PROCEDURE. The V-test of Mackworth is recommended for tactile discrimination as it is both reliable and easy to use.

The apparatus consists of a flat wooden ruler cut in half. The two halves are joined together at one end, and at the other end they are separated by a fixed gap of half an inch. The gap between the two inner edges of the device is therefore anything between 0 millimetres and 13 millimetres, depending on the particular part of the apparatus that is being applied to the tip of the finger. The subjects are required to indicate whether pressure is being applied at one or at two points.

Subjects are tested one at a time and are first given practice on the test. Room temperatures of 60° F–75° F are recommended for the normal estimation of tactile discrimination. Ten threshold readings are normally obtained and these are then averaged to give the tactile discrimination reading.

1.4.3   REFERENCE. The following publication ought to be carefully studied before undertaking any tests of tactile discrimination.
MACKWORTH N.H. (1953) Finger numbness in very cold winds. *J. Appl. Physiol.,* **5**, 533–543.

2   ADAPTIVE PERCEPTIVE INTEGRATION

2.1   **Intersensory transfer.** The concept of intersensory transfer is based on Sherrington's view that in the evolution of the CNS a close interaction has been built up between the various sensory modalities. It can therefore be defined as the integration of distinct sensory inputs to convey consistent meaning. This aspect of perceptual function has a two-fold interest for H.A. projects. Particular life experiences may have a specific effect on perceptual integration, leading to a predominance of the visual over the kinaesthetic sense, for example. This phenomenon which is a manifestation of what is known as field dependence, may have come about because the natural habitat has placed a premium on the use of the visual sense. It can also be a consequence of certain child rearing practices.

In the second place, intersensory transfer may be disturbed as a result of central nervous impairment. When investigating the effects of malnutrition, tropical diseases, heatstroke and the like, inter-sensory transfer tests may provide indications of psychologically significant brain damage which it might be difficult to discover by other means. It must be emphasised, however, that there is at present no sure way whereby deviations in perceptual integration can be attributed to brain damage, rather than to personality factors. Ancillary observations are imperative before any inter-pretation can be attempted. These observations would concern in particular the characteristics of the physical environment, the nature of the subsistence economy, child rearing practices and the manner in which parental authority is exercised, as well as a thorough appraisal of any physical and health factors that might have caused brain damage (neurone loss) and any clinical signs of such damage.

2.1.1   ORIENTATION TO THE VERTICAL

Tests of orientation to the vertical in the face of a misleading visual frame of reference can be used to examine the perceptual integration of the visual and kinaesthetic inputs. The information to be derived from this source is informative on the field dependance concept (environment and personality factors) rather than on brain damage.

2.1.1.1   *Equipment.* The portable Rod and Frame Test designed by P.K. Oltman of the Department of Psychiatry at Downstate Medical Center, 450 Clarkson Ave., Brooklyn, N.Y., is recommended for this purpose. The apparatus sells for approximately $190 and can be ordered directly from Darro Products Corporation, 525 Whitehall Street, Lynbrook, New York.

The following administration procedure, set up by Dr Oltman, is normally sent out with the apparatus.*

2.1.1.2   *Procedure.* The apparatus must be on a sturdy table and be level. Before the subject is seated in front of the apparatus, he is instructed as follows:

'In this test we want to find out how well you can determine the upright—the vertical—under various conditions'.

'In this box (PRFT) you will see a square frame and within this frame you will see a rod'.

'It is possible for me to tilt the frame to the left or the right. I can also tilt the rod to the left or right. I can tilt the frame alone or the rod alone; or I can tilt them both at the same time, either to the same side or to opposite sides.'

'When I lower the curtain at the beginning of each trial, I want you to tell me whether the rod and frame are straight up and down—

*Terminology (e.g. "clockwise") and examples (e.g. "flagpole" to illustrate vertical) may have to be modified to suit cultural circumstances.

i.e. vertical—or whether they are tilted. In other words tell me whether the rod and frame are straight with the walls of this room or whether they are tilted'.

'Are there any questions?'

Trial 1. Adjust the frame to 28L and the rod to 28L. Lower curtain. Say to S: 'What is the position of the rod and the frame?' (Record S's response.)

If S says the rod is not vertical, say to him: 'I will now turn the rod slowly until you think it is straight with the walls of this room. As I said, I will turn it slowly, and after each turn, tell me whether it has been turned enough or whether you want it turned some more. Just say "more" or "enough" after each turn. Please make your decisions quickly and don't be too finicky. Which way shall I move the rod to make it vertical—clockwise or counter-clockwise?'

Now move the rod about 3° at a time opposite to the direction in which the S says it is tilted, until he reports 'enough'. Ask the S after he reports the rod vertical: 'Is the rod now vertical—that is, is it straight with the walls of this room? In other words, is it straight up the way the flagpole outside is?'

If the S should now say that he wants the rod moved some more in either direction, do so. Raise the curtain and record the position of the rod and the time.

If on this first trial, the S reports the rod to be straight at the outset, ask him the question: 'Is the rod now vertical, that is, is it straight with the walls of this room?'

In such instance, give the S the instructions concerning the straightening of the rod, as above, on the next trial. If on the next trial, the S again states that the rod is straight at the outset, give him these instructions on the first trial on which he says that the rod is tilted.

Trial 2. Leave the frame at 28L and adjust the rod 28R. Lower the curtain and say to the S: 'Would you tell me now and at the beginning of all subsequent trials whether the rod and frame are straight with the walls of this room, or tilted; and if the rod is tilted, whether the rod should be moved clockwise or counter-clockwise to be made straight'.

If the S asks you to turn the rod, do so until he says 'enough'.

Ask him again: 'Is the rod now vertical—that is, is it straight with the walls of this room?'

Do not ask this question on subsequent trials. Raise curtain. Record adjustment and time. Proceed to the next trials.

Trial 3. Frame 28R Rod 28R.
Trial 4. Frame 28R Rod 28L.
Trial 5. Frame 28L Rod 28L.
Trial 6. Frame 28L Rod 28R.
Trial 7. Frame 28R Rod 28R.
Trial 8. Frame 28R Rod 28L.

Before S enters the room, be sure frame is straight and curtain up.

If at any time after the rod has been adjusted on a given trial the S should say that he wants it moved some more in either direction, do so.

If the S should take more than 5 seconds on any trial before saying 'more' or 'enough' tell him: 'Please make your decisions quickly'.

If the S should repeatedly say 'more' or 'enough' before the turn of the rod is completed, say to him: 'Please wait until I have completed the turn'.

Check from time to time to determine whether the S's head is in the proper position in the head rest. Attaching the elastic cord around the back of S's head is recommended.

2.1.1.3   *Ancillary Information.* The following ancillary information ought to be obtained for all subjects tested on the Rod and Frame Test.

(a) age, (b) sex, (c) level of education, (d) nature of courses taken at school, i.e. technical vs. non-technical, (e) nature of child-rearing practices followed by the particular ethnic group or sub-culture to which the subject belongs. How harsh or permissive is the parental control of the children in this particular ethnic group or sub-culture? (f) personal history of subject: what was his relationship with his mother and father? How protective was the home environment? What scope for independence did the child receive? Did his (her) mother foster or inhibit his (her) growth? (g) any history of brain damage or head injury? (h) any history of psycho-pathology, including alcoholism? (i) any signs of compulsive eating or obesity?

2.1.1.4 *Reference*
WITKIN H.A., DYK R.B., FATERSON G.E., GOODENOUGH D.R. &
KARP S.A. (1962) *Psychological Differentiation*. New York,
Wiley.

2.1.2 BIRCH INTERSENSORY MODALITY TEST

2.1.2.1 *Rationale*. This test is intended to provide an index of children's
cognitive development from a measurement of the degree of intersensory functioning. The test has been used in nutritional studies,
but may require adaptation for use in cross-cultural studies.

2.1.2.2 *Material and Procedure*. The test material consists of 8 of the
variously shaped blocks of the Seguin-Goddard Formboard which
are presented either visually, 'haptically' or kinaesthetically. In
haptic perception the subject feels the block through a curtain but
cannot see it. In kinaesthetic perception the subject's hand, holding
a stylus, is guided round a series of linocut outlines of the blocks.
The stimuli are presented one at a time through one of the three
modalities and have to be matched or identified with the same or
different shapes in each of the other modalities.

The number of errors made by American children of 5 to 11
years have been published, and the test has given interesting results
on mental development among, for example, Latin American
peasant children and Zambian children in the age range 6–9 years.
However, there seem to be no detailed studies of the relation of
test scores to general intelligence or other recognised ability factors.

2.1.2.3 *References*
BIRCH H.G. & LEFFORD A. (1963) Intersensory Development in
Children, *Monogr. Soc. Res. Child Devel.*, **28,** No. 89.
BIRCH H.G. & LEFFORD A. (1967) Visual Differentiation, Inter-
sensory Integration and Voluntary Motor Control, *Monogr. Soc.
Res. Child Dev.*, **32,** No. 110.

2.2 Embedded Figures Test

2.2.1 RATIONALE AND MATERIAL. This test is directed towards the
measurement of field dependence and the integration of cognitive

and personality components in perception. It is of particular interest for the appraisal of the effects of differential child rearing practices on personality structure. The task set by the test is to hold in mind a simple line figure or shape and to pick it out from within the distracting context of a more complex line figure. The drawings used for this purpose were originally designed by Gottschaldt. The figures were reproduced by Thurstone for a test used in his factorial studies of perception. N.I.P.R. based their Gottschaldt Figures Test, used for the exploration of perceptual abilities, on the Thurstone version. This test is obtainable, with administration manual, from the Director, N.I.P.R. P.O. Box 10319, Johannseburg.

It is rather difficult to get across to persons who are not sophisticated in test performance, but Witkin's version, known as Embedded Figures Test, has been used successfully with Eskimo, Canadian Indian Metis, and a number of African ethnic groups. Harrison Gough, in the Sixth Mental Measurements Yearbook, praises Witkin's test for its 'firm anchoring in a systematic context of theory and empirical evidence', the importance of this particular approach to cognitive testing, and its 'exciting potentialities . . . for cross-cultural usage'. Its diagnostic implications he considers to be related to (a) field independence; (b) cognitive clarity; (c) an analytic versus global perceptual mode, and (d) a general disposition to articulate and structure experience. There is, unfortunately, no manual for the test, but information on its use and testing materials can be obtained directly from Witkin himself (Prof. Herman A. Witkin, Dept. of Psychiatry, College of Medicine, State University of New York, 450 Clarkson Avenue, Brooklyn 10003, N.Y., U.S.A.), or from Prof. P. Vernon, Faculty of Education, University of Calgary, Canada. Group versions of the test can be obtained from The Educational Testing Service, Princeton, New Jersey 08540. They have a number of forms available, known as Hidden Figures and Concealed Figures.

2.2.2   REFERENCES

GOTTSCHALDT, KURT (1929) Über den Einfluss der Erfahrung auf die Wahrnehmung von Figuren, II, *Psychologische Forschung,* **XII,** 1–88.

THURSTONE L.L. (1944) *A Factorial Study of Perception*. University of Chicago Press, Chicago, 72–76.

BUROS O.K. (1965) *The Sixth Mental Measurements Yearbook,* The Gryphon Press, Highlands Park, New Jersey. Ref. 89.

WITKIN H.A. (1950) 'Individual Differences in Ease of Perception of Embedded Figures', *Journal of Personality*, **19**, 1–15.

WITKIN H.A. (1961) Cognitive development and the growth of personality, *Acta Psychologia,* **18** (4), 245–257.

WITKIN H.A. *et al.* (1962) *Psychological Differentiation*. New York, John Wiley & Sons Inc.

2.3   Perception of Geometric Illusions

2.3.1   RATIONALE. The effect of the natural habitat on the way one perceives the world around one has been studied through the medium of geometric illusions. Those who grow up in a largely unstructured natural environment, relatively lacking in clearcut pattern or visual simplicity (e.g. closed-in forest vs. open desert country) or in the artifacts of civilisation (the 'carpentered' world or city scene) appear to have developed differential responses towards shapes, particularly their graphical representation. This would appear to affect the way they perceive certain well-known illusions, such as the Müller-Lyer, the Sander Parallelogram and the Horizontal Vertical Illusion.

Interpretations of this phenomenon are still inconclusive; but the significance of the physical environment for perceptual learning and the subsequent perceptual skills of peoples reared in different habitats suggests that this may prove to be an important research domain for cross-cultural H.A. studies.

The materials and procedures developed by Herskovits, Campbell and Segall have been tried out in a wide range of cultures and have been found usable even with the most primitive of subjects. For further information, application should be made to Prof. D.T. Campbell, Dept. of Psychology, Northwestern University, Evanston, Illinois, U.S.A.

2.3.2   REFERENCES

SEGALL M.H., CAMPBELL D.T. & HERSKOVITS M.J. (1963) 'Cultural Differences in the Perception of Geometric Illusions', *Science*, **139,** 769–771.

CAMPBELL D.T. (1964) *Distinguishing Differences of Perception from Failures of Communication in Cross-Cultural Understanding: Epistemology in Anthropology.* ed. Northrop *et al.*, Wenner-Gren Foundation, New York, pp. 308–336.

SEGALL M.H., CAMPBELL D.T. & HERSKOVITS M.J. (1966) *The influence of culture on visual perception.* Bobbs-Merrill Co. Inc., Indianapolis, U.S.A.

2.4   Form Perception Tests

2.4.1   RATIONALE. Form perception tests are concerned with spatial relations and require an appreciation on the part of the subject of the shape, size and orientation of a number of different parts or pieces that together make up a specified configuration. One or more pieces must be rotated, turned or inverted according to directions concerning the nature and order of manipulations. Subject must be able to visualise the effects of manipulations on position, location and appearance of the pieces, with reference to a particular end state. Knowledge of whether the end state has been achieved satisfactorily is normally apparent in that the subject works through the manipulatory process until he completes the solution.

2.4.2   EQUIPMENT AND PROCEDURE

Form perception tests generally involve the use of form boards which are difficult and expensive to construct. The Form Perception Test of the National Institute for Personnel Research is an exception in this regard. It is a printed test and the pieces made of paper, are pasted down by the subjects. The test is relatively cheap and easy to administer to illiterate peoples. It can be used in group situations. A manual for administering and scoring the test is available. Enquiries should be directed to the Director, National Institute for Personnel Research, P.O. Box 10319, Johannesburg, Rep. of South Africa.

The Form Boards Test of the National Institute for Personnel Research can also be considered for us in H.A. Projects. The National Institute for Personnel Research has developed a very durable series of graded form boards, which can be used, either individually or in small groups. This series has been extensively applied to African samples and has proved particularly useful cross-culturally because it can be administered by means of a silent film. Materials and administration manual are obtainable from N.I.P.R.

2.5 **Perceptual Speed.** The speed with which visual information can be processed is of the utmost importance in adapting to many of the requirements of contemporary life and possibly also for survival in certain primitive cultures. This is particularly true of man-machine systems, where both a high degree of vigilance and the rapid integration of information are essential for the process of decision making. Speed of perception, as part of the individual's personal tempo, can be partly temperamentally, partly culturally determined. In any attempt either to study genotypical components in behaviour, or to trace cultural determinants, perceptual speed tests are likely to be useful, even though the relative importance of either as determinants of a particular behaviour characteristic may be difficult to measure.

The administration of speed tests presents considerable cross-cultural measurement problems, because personal tempo may be naturally slow as part of the total cultural behaviour pattern. Whether the test situation and instructions can change habitual mental set towards maximum effort to speed up responses and whether such effort might bring about a disintegration in perceptual responses it is not possible to say.

Tests that have proved effective in cross-cultural measurement, in that scores yield a broad range of individual differences in speed of performance, are the two sorting tests (Mechanical objects, such as nails, screws, washers and the like to be sorted according to detailed characteristics into a number of classes; metal discs to be sorted according to letters and digits engraved upon them) of the General Adaptability Battery of the N.I.P.R. These tests are particularly suitable for subjects with a low level of scholastic education. A disadvantage is that they measure motor as well as perceptual speed. Equipment, a silent film for test administration and a manual are obtainable from N.I.P.R.

A more purely perceptual test containing also a memory component is the adaptation of Kim's Game developed by Ord and included in the New Guinea Performance Scale. For details of this test, materials and manual, application should be made to: Australian Council for Educational Research, Frederick Street, Hawthorn, Victoria, Australia, 3122. It is known as Observation Test.

2.6   Elithorn's Perceptual Maze
Fairly complex judgements may have to be made when processing incoming visual information. One alternative course of action has to be weighed against another before a decision can be made on which would be more appropriate. This introduces an element of intellectual power, as well as of perceptual speed. Elithorn's Perceptual Maze is such a test, which is nevertheless dealt with here, rathei than in the next section on Higher Mental Processes because it is likely that the major portion of the variance will be accounted for by a perceptual factor or factors, rather than by a logical reasoning process.

2.6.1   RATIONALE. The test consists of a number of target dots superimposed upon the intersections of a lattice background shaped as an inverted triangle or diamond. The subject's task is to find a path along this lattice which passes through the greatest number of target dots. There are two restrictions: the subject may not cut across from one lattice path to another; at each intersection the subject may fork left or right, but must not double back. There is generally more than one 'best' pathway and the subject is said to succeed if he finds anyone of these.

Originally devised to measure the effect of frontal lobe damage, it was found to be relatively sensitive to cerebral damage generally. There are marked differences in performance between male and female subjects and a decline in the ability to solve the maze with age. Initial performance on the test correlates more highly with spatial ability than practised performance and more with spatial skills in boys than in girls. There is some evidence that in groups homogeneous for intellectual skills the test tends to measure personality variables. Though much of this is subject to further replication, and little is known about the cross-cultural use of the test, it nevertheless commends itself for experimental application in H.A. projects. No language responses appear to be involved in solving the maze problems it presents and its structure lends itself to detailed analysis of the strategies employed in achieving solutions. Its apparent sensitivity to brain damage holds out some promise that its determinants will be closer to physiologally than to culturally determined functions. It can also be constructed by computer methods.

2.6.2   MATERIAL AND PROCEDURE
There are two versions, each consisting of 3 demonstration and 18 test patterns. The time taken for each pattern is recorded, one point being scored for a solution within one minute, and an additional point for a solution within 30 secs. The test can be administered either with or without information as to the maximum number of circles which can be achieved in each pattern, and either as an individual or as a group test. Although not yet published as a standardised test, the material has been made freely available to research workers in many parts of the world, and can be obtained, with manual, from the Medical Research Council, Department of Psychological Medicine, Royal Free Hospital, Lawn, Road, London, NW3.

2.6.3   REFERENCES
ELITHORN A. (1955) 'A preliminary report on a perceptual maze test sensitive to brain damage'. *J. Neurol. Neurosurg. Psych.*, **18**, 287–292.

ELITHORN A., *et al.* (1960) 'A Group Version of a perceptual maze test', *Brit. J Psychol.*, **51** (1), 19–26.

2.7   **Perception of Time**
Fraisse (1963) stresses the importance of change in the perception of time. 'Man lives amidst change'. Even before he becomes aware of the fact that he himself is changing, he sees continuous changes

in the world around him. Night succeeds day, good weather follows bad; winter comes after summer. Animals are born and die; nothing can stop the flow of the river or erosion of rock. Everything is caught up in this change, even man. His biological, psychological and social life consists entirely of change' (Fraisse, p. 1).

A number of experiments have been carried out on the relationship between time perspective and time estimation. They were initiated by a study on impulse control in delinquents by Siegman (1961). From this emerged the hypothesis that the longer the range of a subject's future-time perspective, the more rapidly will time seem to pass. This hypothesis was confirmed by Siegman (1961) (a) and (b); (1962) and Geiwitz (1965).

Cultures are differently oriented to time and differences in time perspective would seem to lead to differences in time estimation. It is therefore of the utmost importance to consider cultural-background factors in studies on time perception.

Doob (1960) found that, among the Ganda, those who were more highly acculturated (westernized) were able to estimate time more accurately. Doob argues that, because Westerners have to co-ordinate their activities precisely by a watch, they can improve their judgements of intervals. In contrast, people in less civilized societies often do not have to coordinate their activities too precisely. They provide temporal cues to one another; the chief, for example, has the drums sounded long before a ceremony begins, and hence each person can go about his affairs until he hears the signal. In the absence of timepieces less civilized peoples are less likely to have at hand a convenient and invariant criterion, and thus their time estimates will not be so accurate.

Schwitzgebel (1962) confirmed the hypothesis that certain perceptual organizations are characteristic of cultural groups. He found that Dutch adults were more accurate in their time estimations than Zulu adults. He also found that Zulu men tended to underestimate time intervals consistently.

There is no way of getting an absolute measure of the time experience of an individual. His judgement cannot be separated from the method of expression. The history of experimentation in this field has shown how different methods of time judgement tend to show different degrees of accuracy and reliability. It has been found that verbal estimates are reliable but that reproduction of time is not. Siegman (1962) obtained reliability coefficients of ·82 (5 seconds interval) and ·84 (20 seconds interval) by the method of verbal estimation. By contrast he found coefficients of ·59 and ·40 respectively using the method of reproduction (his subjects reproduced auditory signals by depression of a key).

Clausen (1950) obtained reproduction reliabilities of the same order. For this reason most studies of time judgement have been confined to verbal estimates of time.

Verbal estimations, however, are not suitable for use in cross-cultural contexts. Clock-time might well be meaningless to certain cultural groups. Non-verbal methods, such as the methods of reproduction, however, do not necessarily rely on differences in conception of time.

Du Preez (1963) explored the possibilities of a method designed by Danziger. This method is based on the known reliability of the speed of limb-movements. The method is essentially as follows:

The subject is asked to move a handle horizontally across a frame in such a way that the duration of his movement equals, in his judgement, the duration of a time signal. He makes the movement after the time signal has ceased. The duration and distance of the subject's movement, made at his own speed, are then recorded and analysed.

Du Preez compared various methods of reproduction. He obtained judgements of time by free linear arm movement, controlled linear arm movement, by key-pressing and by gripping the stationary handle. He found that the method of reproduction of time signals by either free or controlled linear movement is more reliable than the method of reproduction by key-pressing and is of the same order of reliability as the verbal estimation of time. The average reliability coefficient he obtained was ·71.

Techniques for the measurement of perception of time have not yet emerged from the research stage, particularly in so far as cross-cultural measurement is concerned. No procedure is sufficiently well standardised to warrant recommendation. Those interested in carrying out time perception studies in the course of H.A. projects are referred to the following references.

CLAUSEN S. (1950) 'An evaluation of experimental methods of time judgement'. *J. exp. Psychol.*, **40**, 756–761.

DANZIGER L. & DU PREEZ P.D. (1963) Reliability of Time Estimation by the Method of Reproduction. *Perc. & Motor Skills*, **16**, 879–884.

DOOB L.W. (1960) *Becoming more civilised: a psychological exploration.* New Haven: Yale University Press.

DU PREEZ P.D. (1963) Relation Between Verbal Estimation and Reproduction of a Short Time Interval: Preliminary Study. *Perc. & Motor Skills*, **17**, 45–46.

FRAISSE P. (1963) *The Psychology of Time.* New York. Harper & Row.

GEIWITZ P.J. (1965) 'Relationship between future time perspective and time estimation'. *Percept. & Motor Skills*, **20**, 843–844.

SCHWITZGEBEL R. (1962) 'The performance of Dutch and Zulu adults on selected perceptual tasks'. *J. soc. Psychol.*, **57**, 73–77.

SIEGMAN A.W. (1962) 'Intercorrelation of some measures of time estimation'. *Percept. & Motor Skills*, a, **14**, 381–382.

SIEGMAN A.W. (1962) 'Future-time perspective and the perception of duration'. *Percept. & Motor Skills*, b, **15**, 609–610.

SIEGMAN A.W. (1961) 'The relationship between future time perspective, time estimation and impulse control in a group of young offenders and in a control group'. *J. consult. Psychol.*, **25**, (6) 470–475.

6

Higher Mental Processes

PRECAUTIONS TO BE TAKEN IN MEASUREMENT

In the measurement of higher mental processes it is more than ever essential to recognise that there are no tests which measure basic intellectual functions independently of the cultural context within which these functions developed. An individual's performance on mental tests, though no doubt ultimately limited by genetic or constitutional factors, always reflects the extent to which his family and society have provided relevant experience and reinforcement which help or hinder the growth of the component skills. Thus it is particularly important to interpret any observation or measurement in the light of cultural background data, as outlined in Chapter II. Some of the requirements need to be specially underlined for testing higher mental processes.

The pronounced heterogeneity of most ethnic groups on the variables involved in higher mental processes makes it essential that population samples be obtained. This raises both questions of number and of sample stratification. Given rather 'narrow-band' or homogeneous groups, it is usually possible to demonstrate statistically significant differences between contrasted samples of, say, 50 each; but it is hardly worth attempting to make comparisons of sets of mental measurements if the numbers fall much below this, unless the cases are carefully matched. A better approach, with more heterogeneous samples, is that based on factorial design and analysis of variance, where the testees are graded and cross-classified on each of the major identifiable parameters, so that the problem of sampling becomes one of picking individuals at random to fit each of the cells in the design. The design will vary according to the purpose of the particular investigation and no general prescription can be given.

Testing at higher mental levels raises fewer problems of equipment, expensive materials, mobile vans, etc. than in other areas.
The general precaution must be taken that when groups of individuals are tested, testees must be screened from each other to
prevent copying. The provision of suitably trained personnel for
test administration is essential. For group tests it will generally be
sufficient for tester to be word perfect in giving test instructions,
to know how to check whether the testees have understood the
instructions, and how to deal with questions. For individual testing,
the tester must have been specifically trained in the particular
procedures. This type of testing is highly skilled and very time
consuming.

**2   WHICH ASPECTS OF BEHAVIOUR SHOULD BE
          TESTED?**

A distinction has previously been drawn between skills which
people acquire for survival and every-day living, and skills whose
acquisition is stimulated by cultural change. This distinction also
holds at the higher mental level. In studying the former, tests will
be of little help and the main need is to observe and record carefully
how a society solves its own problems, what kinds of thinking seem
to be involved in coping with agricultural, hunting or social-conflict
situations; also what persons, with what status, tend to act as
innovators and as obstructors of change. A trained psychologist is
likely to be useful in such surveys as being more aware what to
look for, and what errors are liable to arise in uncontrolled observations. When interest is focussed on the adaptability of a group to
cultural change, or of individual members to education, training,
etc., the higher mental processes become so complex that there is a
strong case for trying to obtain an overall quantitative assessment
of reasoning abilities by applying tests, i.e. by setting people sample
problems. However, success at any such test is affected not only by
the background factors already listed, but also by the compre-
hensibility or unfamiliarity of the test materials. This aspect has
been fully discussed in Chapter 1 and need not be repeated here.

Some psychologists would advocate treating such tests as learning tasks and either recording progress on successive presentations, or not accepting the scores until the testees have approached their asymptote. In our view this approach is less appropriate at the higher mental process level than at the psychomotor. If the mechanics of the material are suitably simplified, a limited amount of explanation and practice produces most of the possible gain. Moreover it is known that scores based on gains with practice are less reliable and valid as predictors of success in education or performance in every-day life than scores based on test performance after a necessary minimum of practice.

3   TESTS OF GENERAL MENTAL ABILITY

There is still considerable conflict of opinion among psychologists about the best single measure of general mental ability, the capacity to perceive new relations which is the central cognitive feature of adaptability. Some consider that there is no single unitary determinant of this general ability, that it breaks up into a number of independent primary abilities with unique features in the perceptual, verbal, numerical reasoning domains. Others hold that important though the latter may be, they are not wholly independent and that a common thread holds them together which can be identified as the power of the mind, that which ultimately determines how well people can solve problems by a process of reasoning. This element can unquestionably be demonstrated to exist and to be present as a general factor in the statistical analyses of batteries of so-called general ability tests. For the purposes of the I.B.P., it is this entity that it will generally be most important to measure. There is some reason to believe that its magnitude depends on the state of development and integrity of the cerebral cortex, which makes it a particularly useful criterion for assessing damage caused by malnutrition or anoxia, or arrested development caused by gross deficiencies in the formative influences provided by the environment.

All available tests are factorially complex, but the general intellectual factor (g) is a more powerful determinant of performance in some than in others.

Two tests that have repeatedly proved their worth, as measures of (g), in vastly different cultures are Raven's Progressive Matrices Test and Kohs Blocks Test.

Both tests are strongly recommended for what are referred to as 'primary activities' in Weiner's Guide to the Human Adaptability Proposals, that is major projects in which from the psychological point of view an overall measure of mental power is a central and essential feature. Results will generally be more reliable if more than one test can be used, and though Progressive Matrices and Kohs Blocks have a considerable overlap, it is nevertheless thought advisable to use one as confirmation of the measures obtained from the other.

3.1   Progressive Matrices

3.1.1   RATIONALE. This is a test of problem solving in which non-verbal, figurative problems are set. The principle on which the figurative matrix is constructed can be deduced from the design that is presented to the testee. When he has discovered the principle, the testee is able to select the missing portion of the design from a number of possible alternatives. Although the test is far from being 'culture-free', it is less affected than more conventional 'intelligence tests' by amount of education, socio-economic status, specific cultural association. Numerous factorial studies have shown that its factorial content is rather complex. More than one kind of reasoning is involved in it, and it may also test perceptual closure and speed, though these would be minor factors. Its meaning is likely to vary with sex and age.

3.1.2   TEST MATERIAL
Most commonly used for group administration is the black and white Standard Form (1938 Version) revised in 1956. It is suitable for subjects aged 12 and upwards who have had a minimum of two years schooling, though it has been successfully used as far down the age scale as 6 years. At these lower levels individual administration is desirable. A coloured version (C 47) first published in 1947 and revised in 1956 has been found easier to use for subjects with no test sophistication and little exposure to western civilisation.

For **group administration** the most appropriate age range is 8–11 with at least 2 years schooling; individual administration 5 years upward without schooling. This version is also applicable to senescents. The test is available from H.K. Lewis Ltd., Gower Street, London, or from the Psychological Corporation, 304 East 45th Street, New York 10017.

3.1.3   TESTING PROCEDURE

Full details on procedures can be obtained from Raven J.C. *Guide to the Standard Progressive Matrices* (H.K. Lewis or Psychological Corporation 1960) and Raven J.C. *Guide to using the Coloured Progressive Matrices* (same publishers, 1960).

In the case of subjects whose level of education is low, or who are relatively unfamiliar with printed materials, and where there are communication difficulties, special precautions need to be taken to make sure that test requirements are understood. It is recommended that a flannelboard or plastiboard technique be used, with work items demonstrating the four major item types. These four types are: (a) attending to the horizontal and vertical dimensions of a pattern; (b) constructing the solution to a simple symmetric figural analogy; (c) discovering an addition or subtraction principle; (d) discovering the principle to the non-symmetric matrix and producing a generally inductive solution, *actually building up the matrix before the group's eyes*. Particular attention should be paid to the horizontal and vertical agreement of the matrix. This should be followed by reinforcement of each item type as it is demonstrated, finally ending with a mixture of types to prevent or discourage sets. Experimenters should notice that if this procedure is used instead of the standard procedure, means will rise and variance decrease. Time limits for the test should be generous (not less than 30 minutes). In the record of procedures followed in applying the test, the actual time limit used *must* be given. The effect of this should be to reduce irrelevant variance.

Because the task of recording answers is often a difficult one for semi-literate or illiterate groups, a number of proctors should be used—one to every six to eight testees to mark individual answer sheets after the answer is pointed out in the booklet. To test a group of 30, some half-dozen assistants might be necessary unless one could make the Raven booklets expendable and adopt a single cross-out procedure.

With school children who have had at least three years in school, recording answers in a simple form should not be too difficult, but the experimenter should establish this before beginning any large scale study. Vernacular translation of instructions is possible, but these should be checked by back translation.

3.1.4   TREATMENT OF DATA

Test score is the total of correct solutions. Norms for the interpretation of scores are available for British adults and children. Many publications give results for different ethnic groups. In each case, however, these standards are relative to the particular testing procedure that has been used. This applies in particular to time limits and to demonstrations that go beyond what was stipulated in the Raven Manual.

When the experiment is only concerned with the comparison of an experimental and control group, the need for population norms does not arise. But if more is needed than the establishment of a significant difference such as a statement of amount of retardation or advancement in a particular population as compared with a reference group, norms are essential. This also applies when one is concerned with the ability of individuals. It is inadvisable to use the same norms for culturally distinct populations.*

3.2   **Kohs Block Design Test**

3.2.1   RATIONALE

There are many adaptations of this test, to meet the characteristics of particular cultural groups, or to make the test more generally applicable cross-culturally. In all of them problem solving takes

* The reader who needs to know more about the factor composition of Progressive Matrices is referred to the following article:

IRVINE S. *How Fair is Culture? Factorial Studies of Raven's Progressive Matrices Across Cultures in Africa*—International Testing Conference, Berlin, 1967, and revised version from Educational Testing Service, Princeton, N.J., U.S.A., 1968. (This article quotes numerous other useful references to the test.)

place through the medium of blocks, painted in different colours along the diagonal of one side, which have to be arranged to reproduce a particular pattern. Besides the general intellectual factor, the test also involves perceptual factors, such as spatial judgement.

3.2.2   AVAILABLE VERSIONS

Both the Wechsler Adult Intelligence Scale and Intelligence scale for children, contain versions of the Kohs Blocks Test. For technique of administration of these versions see: Wechsler, D. 'Wechsler Adult Intelligence Scale Manual', New York, Psychological Corporation 1955, pp. 47–48, and Wechsler, D. 'Wechsler Intelligence Scale for children Manual', same publishers, 1949, pp. 77–79. The WAIS Form is suitable for persons aged 15 who have been to school for 2 years; the WISC form for illiterate adults and children aged 8–14 with not less than 2 years schooling. Administration in both cases is individual. Norms are available for both forms, but separate standardisation is recommended for the population within which the test is to be used. Size and composition of the standardisation sample will depend on the scope and purpose of the investigation.

Materials can be obtained from the Psychological Corporation, 304 East 45th Street, New York 10017.

Thirdly, I.G. Ord's adaptation of Kohs Block Designs in the New Guinea Performance Scales has proved effective with subjects who are very low in the scale of acculturation to western requirements. This version goes by the name of Design Construction Test. Instead of blocks, tiles are used to overcome the difficulties experienced by subjects at this acculturation level in manipulating three-dimensional material to produce designs presented in two dimensions only. The method of presentation has been greatly simplified, and Ord's version is therefore recommended for general use whenever testing circumstances are culturally unpropitious.* Application to purchase or to reproduce the Design Construction Test must be made to the Australian Council for Educational Research, Frederick Street, Hawthorn, Victoria, Australia, 1322. As Ord's manual is not at present available in printed form, the

* It can be administered by mime from age 8 onwards.

Chapter 6

procedure to be followed is given in full in the Appendix to this chapter. The S.A. National Institute for Personnel Research has developed a version of Kohs Block Design Test that can be administered to groups. This version is administered by means of a silent motion picture which provides instructions and demonstrations through mime. It has proved most effective in the mass testing of illiterate adult African labourers and provides a very good measure of g for this type of subject. The materials are simple and cheap, but the use of a cine-projector creates problems in field research. However, the film can be replaced by mime. For details, apply to the Director, N.I.P.R., P.O. Box 10319, Johannesburg.

4   ALTERNATIVE TESTS OF GENERAL MENTAL ABILITY

The Progressive Matrices and Kohs Block Design tests, particularly if used together, are fully adequate to provide control of the general intellectual factor in human adaptability experiments undertaken mainly from a biological point of view. If, however, a more thorough-going exploration of the mental ability component in adaptability is needed, supplementary tests may be useful, mainly because, as has already been pointed out, the tests concerned all have different factor components, besides 'g', and also because the use of a battery facilitates factor analysis and may throw light on differences in mental structure related to environmental conditions.

The following supplementary tests are recommended:

4.1   Porteus Maze Test

This is one of the oldest and best established tests for cross-cultural use. It consists of a series of paper mazes of increasing complexity, the task being to trace a way through the maze with a pencil. Factorially the test contains a good deal more than 'g'. Porteus claimed that personality components were also involved in successful performance and that the test therefore gave a better prediction of performance in every day life than conventional verbal tests of intelligence. Both for this reason and because the mechanics of the test are readily understood cross-culturally, its inclusion is recommended in projects where practical effectiveness is an aspect of behaviour to be investigated. The test material is cheap and administration is easy. For further details see Oscar Buros, Sixth Mental Measurements Yearbook 1965, pp. 823–824. Gryphon Press, Highland Park, New Jersey, 08904.

4.2   **Shipley Abstraction Test**
This is a valuable group test of reasoning ability intermediate between the non-linguistic and the obviously educationally-loaded test. It merely requires some familiarity with numbers and the Roman alphabet. In Shipley's original version some items are based on sequences of words; sequences of abstract figures can be substituted. It chiefly involves grasping the principle underlying a series of numbers, letters, etc. and applying this to producing the next number in the series. It has been shown to correlate highly with general mental ability in Africa, among Canadian indigenes and other groups, as well as in western cultures. It is adaptable for field use if writing surfaces are available.

The only available published version is Shipley's own. Alternative forms, suitable for various levels down to 3 years of education can readily be constructed.

Instructions, as given by Shipley, are very simple. Additional demonstration and practice are desirable for non-western groups educated in a western language. Testers will require some additional training if the test has to be applied to barely literate groups.

Norms are available on Shipley's test for American adults and on Vernon's version for English children and adults. Outside these groups, it will be necessary to set up norms specifically for the populations concerned; for certain kinds of investigations, however, norms are not needed. Raw scores can be used as experimental observations in intergroup comparisons.

Research workers who require more information on the Shipley Abstraction Test and its modification for use in developing countries are advised to seek assistance from the Educational and Occupational Assessment Service, Ministry of Labour, Lusaka, Zambia, or from Prof. A. Heron, Institute for Social Research, P.O. Box 900, Lusaka, Zambia.

4.3   **N.I.P.R.'s Form Series Test**
Each item in this test consists of a sequence of symbols which are a compound of a particular size, colour and shape. Only part of the sequence is presented and the testee is required to continue it by selecting the appropriate plastic forms representing the next two symbols from a tray. The items are printed on a sheet of durable paper, fixed to a plywood board by means of double-coated marking tape. The plastic forms chosen to complete the sequence are affixed to the marking tape. The test has been found suitable for application to African adults in traditional communities and with no scholastic education. The test is highly reliable. Its major factorial content concerns the reproduction of patterns by a mental process involving both analysis and synthesis. Much of its factorial content needs, however, to be further determined and for this reason the test is likely to prove most useful in projects where both the biological and psychological aspects of adaptation are the object of research. For permission to use the test, and for material and manual, application should be made to the Director, National Institute for Personnel Research, P.O. Box 10319, Johannesburg.

Full details concerning this test will be published in monograph supplement No. 5 of Psychologia Africana entitled 'The Construction of Non-Verbal Test of Reasoning Ability for African Industrial Workers'. Probable publication date end of 1968, beginning 1969.

4.4   **Elithorn's Perceptual Maze**
Reference has already been made to this test in para. 2.6, Chapter 5. Although the test is primarily a perceptual speed test, it also involves aspects of higher-level decision making, and as such has a bearing on general intellectual effectiveness. Recent studies with African children have confirmed the wide cultural tolerance of the perceptual maze. A special feature is its low redundancy, the mathematically simple structure of the material allowing a detailed analysis of individual responses to be made by computer programme.

With the N.I.P.R. Form Series Test, it will therefore make a useful addition to a test battery used in supplementary studies involving higher mental processes.

For references, test material, manual and computer programmes, application must be made to the Medical Research Council, 20 Park Crescent, London, W1.

4.5 **Tests with Verbal Content**

Whenever a sizeable proportion of the child population is exposed to education, it may be profitable in many projects, to make use of more educationally-loaded materials. Provided the educational opportunities within the group or groups can be assessed, these tests measure the stage of intellectual development achieved and, indeed, give better predictions of future educability or trainability than most non-verbal materials. There are many American and British models, but it is unlikely that these tests can be used without modification outside the American and British educational systems. It is safer to construct this type of test *de novo* to ensure that their content is in keeping with local educational criteria and methods. The minimal measures in this area might be a test of vocabulary and language usage (i.e. in the language of instruction), and a test of simple arithmetical operations which will, to a greater extent, reflect the success of mechanical drill provided by the education system up to that point.

When this stage of mental development is reached, though not before, it is feasible to use timed tests, and even group tests with machine-scored answer sheets.

Similar comments apply to tests of the conventional verbal intelligence type, many of which have been found useful for testees who have completed primary education, or higher levels. Tests of this type have been successfully employed in educational and vocational selection in Africa. Illustrative examples in the English language medium can be obtained from the National Institute for Personnel Research, P.O. Box 10319, Johannesburg. Research workers are, however, advised to contact local educational authorities and research institutes to ascertain the availability of test instruments.

4.6   **Mechanical-Technical, Clerical and other Vocational Aptitudes**

It is difficult to find vocational aptitude tests which are known to give valid results in a range of ethnic groups, since the applicability of such tests is severely restricted by the amount of relevant experience and opportunity in the group concerned.

Two test batteries can, however, be recommended, namely the General Adaptability Battery (G.A.B.) of the N.I.P.R. and the AID Battery of the American Institute for Research.

The G.A.B. is probably the most extensively used test of its kind anywhere in the world, having been in routine use in Southern and Central Africa for twenty years. Hundreds of thousands of adult workers have been classified by means of this battery for unskilled and semi-skilled occupations. Simple equipment suitable for mass-administration is used (sorting tests, form boards, mechanical assembly tests, block design and construction tests) and the test is unique in that the whole battery can be applied by means of a silent cine-film, which makes it eminently suitable for cross-cultural use. Sets of equipment, or working drawings for the construction of the tests and copies of the test-administration film can be obtained from the National Institute for Personnel Research in Johannesburg.

The AID-AIR tests are intended for more sophisticated subjects, with at least a primary education and for a more varied and higher level occupational classification. Great care has been taken to suit content and test-administration to non-western cultures, particularly those in Africa, where the battery or parts of it, have been used from Algeria down to Zambia. For information about this test series application should be made to the Director, American Institute of Research, 410, Amberson Avenue, Pittsburgh 32, Penn., U.S.A.

5   **TESTS FOR SPECIAL PURPOSES**

Many psychologists would critise the suggestions made above on the grounds that mental capacities, even at fairly primitive levels, are far too varied to be satisfactorily represented by scores on one or two tests of so-called general intelligence or reasoning. It is quite possible to sample a much wider range of fairly distinctive abilities such as reasoning, space, fluency, rote memory, etc.

It would be of particular interest to apply uniform batteries of tests of such abilities to two or more contrasted groups, and to subject them to analysis by accepted factorial procedures. For the most part, however, such tests are suitable at the moment only for quite advanced populations, and they cannot readily be adapted for standardised application to other groups. Moreover, the less advanced the group, generally the greater the degree of communality or overlapping between different tests, and the more representative a general test or battery is likely to be.

APPENDIX TO CHAPTER 6

INSTRUCTIONS FOR ADMINISTRATION

OF ORD'S ADAPTATION OF KOH'S BLOCK DESIGN TEST

MATERIAL:

(A)   Plastic square tiles of three types, as follows:

Six plastic red pieces, $1\frac{1}{4}$ inch square and $3/16$ inch deep.

Six plastic white pieces, $1\frac{1}{4}$ inch square and $3/16$ inch deep.

Sixteen plastic half red and half white pieces bisected on the diagonal, $1\frac{1}{4}$ inch square and $3/16$ inch deep.

(B)   Shallow plastic trays constructed by sticking thin white plastic $1/16$ inch thick on top of light grey plastic of the same dimensions. The tray is formed by having cut out of the white plastic squares of the following dimensions:

Two large enough to contain four plastic squares, loosely fitted.

Two large enough to contain nine plastic squares, loosely fitted. The second is constructed so that the square is presented to the subject diagonally as a diamond.

One large enough to contain sixteen plastic squares, loosely fitted.

(C)   Thirteen different designs, shown in the attached illustration, but of the same proportions as the material. On the illustration a dimension of half an inch equals $1\frac{1}{4}$ inch on the designs and materials.

Subject

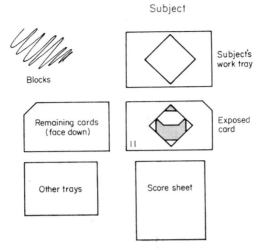

Blocks

Subject's work tray

Remaining cards (face down)

11

Exposed card

Other trays

Score sheet

Tester

(a) **Non scale sketch to illustrate layout of test apparatus, with card 11 exposed.**

(b) **Half size sketch of Card 10.**

10

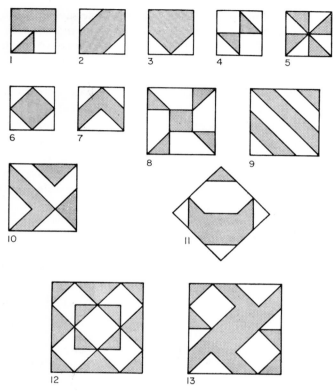

(c) The above designs are to be cut from red paper and mounted centrally on white cards as shown in (b) on the facing page. The designs are to a scale of $\frac{1}{4}$ in. $= 1\frac{1}{4}$ in.

N.B. Designs are shown in positions as seen by tester.

Figure 2. Design construction test. Adaptation of Kohs Blocks Test by I. G. Ord, Chief Psychologist, Public Service Commissioners Dept., Port Moresby, New Guinea, for the New Guinea Performance Scales.

PROCEDURE

Design (1). Empty all the plastic squares on the table saying, '*Look at these pieces: there are three kinds only*'. Pick up and show the subject each of the three different kinds one after the other saying '*Look, there is this kind, all white*', sorting out into a small pile four white pieces, '*This kind, all red*', again sorting out a pile of red pieces, '*and this kind, half red and half white*', likewise sorting out a small pile.

Then say, '*Watch what I do*'. Within one of the small trays arrange the four pieces one at a time slowly to make the design shown on Card (1), without exposing Card (1) to the subject.

Leaving the model intact, place the other small tray in front of the subject and say, '*Now, inside there*', pointing into the tray, '*make one the same as this one*', pointing at the model. If the subject successfully completes the design within the time limit of 60 seconds, score 2 and proceed to Design (2).

If the subject fails to complete the design within the time limit or arranges the blocks incorrectly, pick up his pieces, leaving the examiner's model intact, and say, '*Watch again*'.

Demonstrate a second time using the subject's tray, pause when the design is complete to allow the subject to see the completed design, then empty the tray, mixing up the pieces with the remaining pieces, but still leaving the examiner's model intact and say, '*Now you try again. Make it just like mine*'. Whether the subject succeeds or fails on this trial proceed to Design (2). He scores 1 for success on this second effort.

Reversal or rotation of the design more than 60° is considered an error. However, before giving the second trial say, '*That is not quite right; see, it should go this way*', rotating the design to conform with the model. The tray is then emptied out and the subject invited to make the design again thus, '*Make it the same this time*'. If he persists in his reversal, he is considered to have failed, but if he corrects this reversal, he is given a second trial score of 1 point. The same procedure for reversal is followed for design (2) but not for designs (3) to (12). If there is another reversal in designs (3) to (7) it should merely be pointed out as wrong, but only once more, by rotating the design to conform with the model but not allowing another trial or crediting any score.

Design (2). Remove the tray and pieces that served as model for design (1) and put in their place the card marked (2), saying, *"This time I am going to make this picture."* Make the design slowly in his tray. When completed point first to the design and then to the tray and say, *'See, they are the same'*. Then empty the tray, mixing up the pieces with the remainder and say, *'In here'*, pointing inside the tray, *'Make one just like it. One the same as this'*, pointing to the picture.

If the subject is successful on the trial, score two and proceed to design (3). If he fails, demonstrate a second time, saying, *'Watch me again'*. After making the design, mix up the pieces and say, *'Now try it'*. Whether or not the subject succeeds on the second trial, proceed to design (3). He scores one for success on the second attempt.

Designs (3)—(13). Place the card for the designs before the subject and say, *'Now make one like this. Work as quickly as you can. Tell me when you have finished'*. When the subject indicates he has finished or after the time limit has expired, mix up the pieces and then present the next design.

If the subject does not complete design (3) in the time limit, empty his tray and show him how it is done with the same gestures and comments as applied to design (2). Then empty the tray and let him have a second attempt. If he gets it correct in the time limit at the second attempt, allow him one mark. Do not demonstrate any designs or allow any second attempts after the third one, except with item (7) where, if needs be, you merely demonstrate how it is done without any comment. In item (4) sometimes the white pieces are not inserted by the subject as he does not seem to appreciate that this is part of the design. In this case, point to the white part of the design and empty spaces and say, *'What pieces go here?'*

When design (8) is reached, replace the small tray with the medium sized one, saying, *'This time use nine pieces'*. Again before design (11) is reached, replace with the appropriate tray. Do likewise before design (12) saying, '*This time you will need more pieces*'.

Proceed with item (12) only if the subject has scored on one of items (9)–(11). Similarly, proceed with item (13) only if the subject has scored on item (12). Otherwise discontinue after three consecutive failures to score. If the time limit has expired on any item and the subject has only to insert one more piece to complete the pattern, it is best to allow him to complete it before proceeding to the next item thus avoiding any unnecessary discouragement.

In the case of items (8)–(12) he should, on completion of the item, be scored as if he had completed the item within maximum time limits. In items (12) and (13) he should so be allowed to complete the pattern and score if he has either one or two pieces remaining to complete the design correctly.

Timing of all items commences when the subject first picks up a piece.

Before commencing items (4), (7) and (10), and after displaying the respective designs say, '*Work as quickly as you can*'.

Sometimes, obviously either through lack of manipulative skill or carelessness or even over-willingness to please, a subject completing all earlier pieces of a design correctly, inadvertently inserts the last piece incorrectly, looking up immediately to indicate that he is finished without having bothered finally to check the result of his last insertion. In such a case, without suggesting by tone or gesture that he is necessarily wrong, say, '*Is that the same as the design?*' pointing slowly and deliberately first to his design and then generally to the copy design. If then on checking he immediately and obviously realizes his mistake and corrects it, no marks should be included in his total for the design.

After he makes such a correction, say, '*Next time be more careful*'. If instead he starts major alterations to his design he should be stopped, the design restored to its original state and he be shown where he is wrong, the examiner saying, '*You were nearly right. See this piece*', point to the piece, '*Is wrong. Turn it until it is correct*', and then say, '*See it is now right*'. Pause and then say, '*Next time be more careful*'. Then score the design as it was before it was corrected.

This latter procedure should be followed no more than twice.

SCORING. Scoring is mainly according to the completion of items within time limits. Except for the first two items explained in instructions for administering the test, and the last item, scoring is devised so that an extra credit of one is given if designs are completed in less than half the maximum time limits.

In the case of items (8), (11), (12) and (13) part credits are permitted for near correct answers completed within the time limits. Scoring details are tabulated as follows:

Design	Score (with time limits in seconds)				Correction for Part Scores
	4	3	2	1	
(1)–(2)			0–60		Score 1 for second attempts within time limit.
(3)–(5)			0–30	31–60	Score 1 for second attempts within time limit on item (3) only.
(6)–(7)			0–45	46–90	
(8)		0–60	61–120		Deduct one for each corner piece inserted at the wrong angle.
(9)–(11)		0–90	91–180		In item (11) deduct a mark if centre piece all white or all red and otherwise correct.
(12)	0–120	121–240			Deduct a mark for a wrong piece; or two marks for two wrong pieces if the design still remains symmetrical.
(13)	0–120	121–180	181–240		Deduct two marks for a wrong piece.

Total possible marks—34.

The items and test layout are illustrated in Figure 2 on pages 88–89.

Index of Research Institutes, Publishers of Equipment and Test Material and Standards

Index of Names

Index of Subjects

A GUIDE TO THE
HUMAN ADAPTABILITY PROPOSALS

IBP HANDBOOK No 1

A Guide to the
Human Adaptability Proposals

J. S. WEINER
Convenor, Human Adaptability Section

With a contribution by

PAUL T. BAKER

SECOND EDITION

INTERNATIONAL BIOLOGICAL PROGRAMME
7 MARYLEBONE ROAD, LONDON NW1

BLACKWELL SCIENTIFIC PUBLICATIONS
OXFORD AND EDINBURGH

SBN 632 06080 8

First Published 1965
Second Edition 1969

Printed in Great Britain by
BURGESS AND SON (ABINGDON) LTD
ABINGDON, BERKSHIRE
and bound by
THE KEMP HALL BINDERY, OXFORD

Contents

PUBLISHER'S NOTE

Since going to press we have been notified of a change of
address — see p. 10.

Dr. M.S. Malhotra,
Defence Institute of Physiology and Allied Sciences,
Delhi, Cantt–10, India.

A Guide to the Human Adaptability Proposals

Contents

Foreword

This volume inaugurates a series of IBP Handbooks which will be published as material for them becomes available. Some of the series, such as this, will be general guides to the sectional activities of IBP. Others will be handbooks on methodology, a number of which will result from the symposia which are being held in a good many subjects during Phase I, that is the design and feasibility stage of IBP. It is not intended that the handbook series will contain the actual results of research undertaken under IBP, which would be published more appropriately in standard scientific journals.

The format of the handbooks has been chosen for convenience of transport and cheapness of postage. Since there is some urgency in spreading information around the world, and since some numbers in the series are likely to be of ephemeral value, to be replaced as the IBP programme unfolds, or new and better methods are evolved, speed of publication has been considered more important than perfection. However, within the limits of staff and finance available, every effort has been made to avoid error. The authors of handbooks and the Central and Sectional Offices of IBP are ready to answer any queries which arise.

August 1965

E. B. WORTHINGTON
Central Office of IBP
7 Marylebone Road
London NW1

POSTSCRIPT

This, the first of the IBP handbooks, is also the first to be issued in revised form. For the Human Adaptability section of IBP, two later numbers of the series—No. 9, *Human Biology:* A guide to field methods, edited by J.S. Weiner and J.A. Lourie, and No. 10, *Methods for the measurement of Psycho-*

logical Performance, edited by Dr S. Biesheuvel—will very soon become available. Nevertheless, there continues to be a demand for No. 1, which has been out of print. Therefore Dr Weiner has brought it up to date. Together with the comprehensive classified index to HA projects (*IBP News* No. 19), the basic documentation for this section of IBP is thus completed.

April 1969

E.B.W.

Preface

This Guide to the Human Adaptability part of the International Biological Programme is offered both as a progress report and a blueprint. It sets out the aims, scope and organization of the programme as these have developed up to August 1965 following 3 years of intensive consideration by human biologists from over 30 countries. Naturally, the guide is uneven in the precision with which the proposals are formulated in the different categories of research, but it is hoped that sufficient information is given here to make clear to National Committees and others what is intended in terms of actual research. It should be stressed that the companion volume to this guide will be a 'Handbook of Agreed Methods' now under preparation. The proposals for 'activities in the field' are given only in outline as the agreed techniques and procedures will be presented in the companion volume.

The scope of the Human Adaptability Programme has been endorsed now by human biologists, geneticists, physiologists, epidemiologists, anthropologists and medical scientists from many countries. The objectives of the programme, it is fair to claim, are realistic and eminently worthwhile. Already one can say that the realization of the IBP objectives now lies to a considerable extent with the administrators and politicians, for they have it in their power to make or mar the enterprise of scientists whose work takes them across national boundaries.

To put together this guide I have relied heavily on the contributions, spoken and written, already made to the project by many biologists. The names that appear in the text represent only a proportion of the people who are helping with such goodwill. I have incorporated (sometimes *verbatim*) material from contributions made by a number of colleagues to whom I have been able to appeal urgently because of their close geographical proximity— these include Prof. N.A. Barnicot (Disease and genetic selection); Dr G.A. Harrison (High altitude studies); Dr A. Mourant (Blood group surveys); Dr D.F. Roberts (Demography and congenital defects) and Dr J.M. Tanner (Growth and physique). I am indebted to Professor Lange Andersen (Work-

ing capacity) for his unstinted help. I am particularly grateful to Professor
Paul Baker for preparing as a special contribution to this number a paper on
multidisciplinary studies.

I acknowledge also the detailed advice from members of the H.A.
Sectional Committee and of the Commission for Physiological Anthropometry set up by the International Union of Physiological Sciences (IUPS).

As Convener, I wish here to acknowledge my deep gratitude to all
those colleagues, too numerous to mention by name, who are working
through national groups and national committees, international working
parties and conferences in these years of the International Biological Programme to bring to realization the exciting plans for the study of Human
Adaptability.

August 1965

NOTE ON SECOND EDITION

This second edition of the *Guide to the HA Proposals* has been prepared after
the end of the planning stages of IBP (Phase I). The reason for this is that a
number of countries were not able to set up the appropriate committees until
late in Phase I, and the Convener has continued to receive enquiries about the
planning of projects. The demand for the HA Guide has in fact been such
that the first edition has now been exhausted. This second edition will also,
it is thought, prove useful to the HA Chairmen, HA Correspondents and
Team Leaders, because it contains more up-to-date information. The main
changes in this edition include information on the Handbook of Recommended Methods (HA Handbook No. 9, *Human Biology—a Guide to
Field Methods*, by J.S. Weiner and J.A. Lourie), a list of laboratories which
have expressed readiness to give training in various aspects of human biology
pertinent to the HA programme, an up-to-date list of the HA Consultants,
and also of National HA Chairmen and HA Correspondents. The Index of
all HA projects from the 40 or so participating countries is published separately, as IBP News No 19, and is obtainable from the IBP Central Office,
7 Marylebone Road, London NW1, England.

December 1968

J. S. WEINER
21 Bedford Square
London WC1

1

HA: Human Adaptability Programme

SCOPE

It is fitting that the International Biological Programme should include a section aimed at the world-wide comparative study of human adaptability. The IBP as a whole is concerned essentially with the functional relationship of living things to their environments, in the sea, in fresh water and on the land; it is conceived as a world-wide ecological study of communities of plants and animals: those still existing in relatively natural habitats and those in more disturbed or artificial conditions.

An analogous approach can be made to the ecology of mankind. At this stage of human history vast changes are affecting the distribution, population density, and ways of life of human communities all over the world. The enormous advances in technology make it certain that many communities which have been changing slowly or not at all will relatively soon be totally transformed. We are in a period when the biology of the human race is undergoing continuous change measured in terms of health, fitness and genetic constitution. The International Biological Programme provides a great opportunity to take stock of human adaptability as it is manifested at the present time in a wide variety of terrains, climates and social groups, to deepen our knowledge of its biological basis and to apply this knowledge to problems of health and welfare. To do all this satisfactorily, for communities ranging from the very simple to the highly industrialized, requires an integrated approach and an application of methods drawn from many fields, particularly those of human environmental physiology, population genetics and developmental biology aided by auxiliary disciplines, for example in medicine, anthropology, ecology and demography.

Further discussion of the scope of the programme will be found in the volume *The Biology of Human Adaptability* edited by Paul T. Baker and J.S. Weiner, Clarendon Press, Oxford, 1966.

CATEGORIES OF RESEARCH ACTIVITIES

The problems of human biology which are appropriate for study within the IBP are manifold. At the Paris Assembly of IBP, it was agreed that these should be regrouped and that national contributions to IBP should be selected from amongst the following categories in accordance with the interest and resources of the countries concerned.

Category 1: Survey of sample populations in conformity with a world scheme
The general aim is to carry out as rapidly as possible surveys on a wide geographical range using standardized methods. Surveys are intended to make good as rapidly as possible deficiencies in our present knowledge of the distribution of important population characteristics. A knowledge of the distribution of these characteristics will, in itself, throw light upon many problems of human variability, adaptation and welfare.
- a   Extensive surveys to determine gene frequencies of known polymorphic systems.
- b   Extensive surveys on growth and physique.

Category 2: Intensive multi-disciplinary regional studies based on habitat contrasts
The general aim is to elucidate physiological and genetic processes concerned in adaptation and selection in relation to climatic and other environmental factors which Professor Baker has explored in an incisive and stimulating essay included in this volume. The multidisciplinary approach appropriate to a particular research problem and area would necessarily be based on an integration of the following components:
- i   a basic socio-demographic assessment of the community (for sampling, genetic and other purposes),
- ii   a basic assessment of the environment,
- iii   a general survey of genetic constitution (following Category 1(a) above),
- iv   an assessment of medical status of the subjects,
- v   an assessment of dental condition,
- vi   an assessment of nutritional condition,
- vii   a background description of the daily and seasonal activities,
- viii   an assessment of physique and growth [following Category 1(b) above],
- ix   an assessment of working capacity as an index of fitness,
- x   environmental physiological studies,
- xi   genetic studies.

Every population chosen is to be studied if possible by this comprehensive multi-disciplinary approach. The particular problems of interest will determine which elements are to receive special and sustained attention. The studies may be grouped for convenience as studies with emphasis on:

a environmental physiology,
b high altitudes,
c genetic constitution,
d nutrition,
e growth and physique,
f fitness (working capacity and respiratory function).

Clearly, certain of the special investigations of Category 3 could find a place in these multi-disciplinary studies.

Category 3: Special investigations on selected populations

A number of problems requiring intensive study but on a less comprehensive basis than that of Category 2 have been selected for the consideration of national committees.

a Studies of physiological fitness (working capacity and pulmonary function) of particular population samples, as far as possible on a longitudinal basis. Three groups in particular are of interest:
    i samples from urban industrialized populations,
    ii samples from non-industrialized populations,
    iii athletes.
b disease as a selective agent of genetic constitution.
c particular socio-demographic factors affecting genetic constitution.
d factors controlling population dynamics. (This proposal has still to be formulated in detail but aspects are included in b and c),
e special nutritional problems. (FAO has placed particular emphasis on 'calorie intake in different habitats'.)

Category 4: Investigations related to current WHO activities

It seems feasible in many cases to include in the above Categories certain observations which are complementary to current WHO interests, for example:

a surveys of blood pressure in relation to age, sex and occupation,
b haematological data (total red cell counts, etc.),
c antibody levels in blood,
d certain blood constituents (e.g. phospholipids, plasma proteins),
e congenital defects using a standard check list.

PHASE I (1964-1967)

   i   methodology, leading to production of the Handbook of Agreed Methods,

  ii   research required for establishing the methodology,

 iii   training programme,

 iv   formulation of the definitive programmes for Phase II,

  v   pilot, design and feasibility studies.

PHASE II (1967-72)

During Phase II the survey work and multi-disciplinary regional studies as laid down under the 4 Categories of Research (*IBP News No.* 9) will be carried out, by national (or multi-national) teams in accordance with their national programmes.

2

Guide notes on phase I

METHODOLOGY

A major aim of Phase I was the production of a Handbook of Recommended Methods for use in the HA Section. This Handbook is now available (J.S. Weiner and J.A. Lourie: IPB Handbook No. 9, *Human Biology: A Guide to Field Methods*, 1969). In it some 50 separate procedures are described covering a wide range of enquiry essential to the biological study of human populations.

The techniques described in this Handbook are based on contributions made by some 100 human biologists, expert in their own fields. Nearly all the techniques have been the subject of discussions at scientific conferences, seminars or working groups and they have been submitted by the contributor himself or by the Convener of the Human Adaptability Section to other authorities in the particular field. It can be claimed, therefore, that a large measure of agreement has been reached in formulating the procedures in the Handbook. It should, however, be stressed that these methods are to be regarded only as *recommendations* as the basis for projects within IBP. It is hoped that the great majority of investigators will find it possible to include these procedures in their investigations even if they decide to use additional or alternative methods, appropriate for any special objectives they have in mind. In this way one of the major aims of IBP—a high degree of comparability between studies of different populations—will be achieved.

The Contents are as follows:

A   GROWTH AND PHYSIQUE
A1   Anthropometry
A2   Puberty rating
A3   Photogrammetry
A4   Radiographic measurements
A5   Body density by underwater weighing

B   GENETIC CONSTITUTION
B1   Blood collection and subdivision
B2   Transport of blood specimens

Chapter 2

B3   G6PDD testing in the field
B4   Testing for acetylator phenotype in the field
B5   Detection of foetal red cells in maternal blood (Kleihauer technique)
B6   Phenylthiocarbamide (P.T.C.) taste-testing in the field
B7   Tests on saliva and urine
B8   Cytogenetics
B9   Colour-confusion charts for testing colour vision
B10 Tests of colour vision by anomaloscope
B11 Skin colour measurement by spectrophotometry
B12 Dermatoglyphics
B13 Morphological measurements in genetic studies
B14 Dentition
B15 Anthroposcopy

C WORK CAPACITY AND PULMONARY FUNCTION
C1   Indirect measurement of maximum aerobic power
C2   Direct measurement of maximum aerobic power
C3   Aerobic power
C4   Forced expiratory volume and vital capacity
C5   Morphological measurements in work capacity and pulmonary studies
C6   Assessment of habitual physical activity
C7   Tests with dynamometers
C8   Simple performance tests

D CLIMATIC TOLERANCE
D1   Whole body cold tolerance sleeping test
D2   Whole body cold tolerance waking test
D3   Cold-induced pressor test
D4   Cold-induced vasodilatation test
D5   Controlled-hyperthermia heat tolerance test
D6   Multi-stress heat tolerance test (multiple exposures)
D7   Multi-stress heat tolerance test (single exposure)
D8   A mobile hot-room for field use
D9   Salt and water studies
D10 Sweat-gland counting
D11 Thermal comfort assessments
D12 Morphological measurements in relation to climatic studies

E NUTRITIONAL STUDIES
E1   Assessment of human nutritional status
E2   Household food intake survey
E3   Individual food intake by weighing
E4   Recall questionnaire on kinds and frequencies of foods eaten (non-quantitative)

F MEDICAL AND METABOLIC STUDIES
F1 General medical examination
F2 Continued morbidity survey
F3 Blood pressure determinations
F4 Haematological, immunological, and other serological tests
F5 Thyroid and related studies
F6 List of congenital defects

G DEMOGRAPHIC ASSESSMENT AND
   RELATED SOCIO-CULTURAL FACTORS
G1 Demographic and related data
G2 Socio-demographic studies in relation to female reproductive performance

H ENVIRONMENTAL DESCRIPTION
H1 Habitat in general

A second smaller and specialized methodology handbook is also available. This is IBP Handbook No. 10, *Methods for Measurement of Psychological Performance*, edited by S. Biesheuvel. 1969.

TRAINING

The HA Sectional Committee has recommended that training should normally be in the form of Postgraduate Fellowships held for a year, during which time the Fellow would receive instruction in specific methods appropriate to his interests in the Human Adaptability Project. This instruction should, however, form part of an advanced one-year course in the subject (e.g. environmental physiology, genetics, nutrition, etc.) concerned. Many departments would find it possible to accept suitable students for full-time one-year courses. In addition, some institutes may be able to make arrangements for graduates to take short courses, particularly on methodology. Offers to consider the acceptance of students for training courses in various aspects of human biology have been received from the undermentioned laboratories (*see* list). In most cases intending students will need to make their own financial arrangements.

For further information please approach these laboratories and not the Convener.

1 For growth studies

Dr J. Huizinga,
Institute of Human Biology
22–24 Achter den Dom
Utrecht
Netherlands

Dr M. Prokopec,
Institute of Hygiene
Srobárova 48
Prague 10
Czechoslovakia

Professor J.M. Tanner,
Dept. of Growth and Develop-
  ment
Institute of Child Health
30 Guildford Street
London WC1
England

Professor J. Hiernaux,
Centre de Biologie Humaine
Institut de Sociologie
44 avenue Jeanne
Brussels 5
Belgium

Dr M. Ikai,
School of Education
Department of Physical Fitness
University of Tokyo
Hongo, Tokyo, Japan

2 For nutrition

Dr J.V.G.A. Durnin,
Department of Physiology
The University
Glasgow W2

Professor K. Guggenheim
Department of Nutrition
Hebrew University
Hadassah Medical School
Jerusalem, Israel

3 For dental examination

Professor Dr H. Brabant,
Clinique Stomatologique
Hôpital Universitaire Saint-Pierre
Rue Haute 322
Brussels 1
Belgium

4   For population genetics

Professor C.A. Clarke,
Department of Medicine
The University
Liverpool

Professor J. Hiernaux,
Centre de Biologie Humaine
Institut de Sociologie
44 avenue Jeanne
Brussels 5
Belgium

Professor J.V. Neel,
University of Michigan Medical
  School
Department of Human Genetics
1133 E. Catherine Street
Ann Arbor
Michigan
U.S.A.

Dr J. Huizinga,
Institute of Human Biology
22–24 Achter den Dom
Utrecht
Netherlands

Dr E. Goldschmidt,
Laboratory of Genetics
Hebrew University
Jerusalem
Israel

5   For climatic tolerance

HEAT TOLERANCE

Dr R.H. Fox,
Division of Human Physiology
National Institute for Medical
  Research (MRC Laboratories)
Holly Hill
Hampstead, London NW3
England

Dr B. Givoni
Department of Building
  Climatology
Technion
Haifa, Israel

COLD TOLERANCE

Professor Loren Carlson
School of Medicine
University of California at Davis
California 95616
U.S.A.

Dr J.S. Hart,
National Research Council
Ottawa
Ontario
Canada

Climatic Tolerance (Heat Tolerance) continued

Professor W.V. MacFarlane,
Department of Animal Physiology
Waite Agricultural Research
  Institute
P.O. Box 1, Glen Osmond
South Australia 5064.

Dr C.H. Wyndham,
Human Sciences Laboratory
Chamber of Mines Research
  Laboratories
P.O. Box 809, Johannesburg
South Africa

6 For work capacity and pulmonary function

Professor Dr K. Lange Andersen,
School of Physiotherapy
Trandheimsveien 132
Oslo, Norway

Professor Dr P.A. Biersteker
Fysiologisch Laboratory
Rijksuniversiteit
Utrecht
Vondellaan 24
Netherlands

Dr J.E.Cotes,
Pneumoconiosis Research Unit
Llandough Hospital
Penarth
Glamorgan
Wales

Professor H. Denolin
Cardiology Department
University
St. Peter's Hospital
Brussels
Belgium

Professor Dr F. Kreuzer
Department of Physiology
Faculty of Medicine
Kapittelweg 40
University of Nijmegen
Nijmegen, Netherlands

Dr M. Ikai,
School of Medicine
Department of Physical Fitness
University of Tokyo
Hongo, Tokyo, Japan

Dr M.S. Malhotra,
Defence Institute of Physiology
  and Allied Sciences
Madras Medical College
Madras 3, India

Dr V. Seliger,
Department of Physiology
Faculty of Physical Education
  and Sport
Charles University
Ujezd 450, Praha 1
Mala Strana, Czechoslovakia

The HA Consultants will also do their best to give advice on training opportunities. A list of the Consultants is given on page 57.

3

Guide notes on phase II

INTRODUCTION

Although the scope of the HAP was considerably reduced, redefined and regrouped at the July, 1964 Paris IBP Assembly (*IBP News, No.* 2), the programme still covers a very wide field.

The categories of research now put forward (*see* Introduction above) represent the outcome of many discussions and consultations over the three-year period 1962–64, and clearly can be justified on a number of grounds.

The categories were chosen to take account of: (1) the need for urgent international action for the rapid accumulation of certain biological data; (2) the need for a multidisciplinary co-ordinated and sustained approach in certain 'key' habitats for the solution of basic problems; (3) the great variation in scientific personnel and other resources available in different countries; and (4) the relevance of the programme to health and well-being.

The categories have been devised so that the research activities of Phase II can be pursued at two levels—as 'extensive' surveys, by participation in world-wide co-ordinated surveys as laid down, particularly in categories 1, 3a and 4, and as 'intensive' long-term regional studies requiring internationally standardized methods pursued by national or multinational teams, and these are laid down in categories 2 and 3. (Studies made under these last categories would, in most cases, automatically serve the purposes also of categories 1 and 4).

Every endeavour has been made to ensure that HAP is *flexible* in that free choice is given to the different countries participating in the IBP to choose topics from a wide range and that there is *uniformity* and compatability in the proposals in that similar topics will be investigated in different places using standardized methods. In this way, systematic information will be obtained on many aspects of adaptability which can be related, over a wide range, to geographic and climatic conditions, nutrition and disease and other ecological factors. At the same time, new opportunities should be opened up for the study by many laboratories of the mechanisms underlying the processes of acclimatization, physical fitness and genetic selection. It is intended also that many of the investigations will be extended to studies bearing closely on problems of health and welfare.

In elaborating these suggestions, and in order to indicate what is intended in HAP, two aspects require attention.

Firstly, the need has been felt for a survey or *review of our present knowledge* and ideas on human adaptability and ecology to cover the main categories of HAP. An attempt to provide this background material for the major regions of the world was the object of the Wenner-Gren (HA Conference) of June, 1964. The contributions by the 18 authors comprise discussions of physiological, genetic, developmental and anthropological studies of a wide variety of population groups in Africa, India, South West Asia, Australia and New Guinea, South America, the circumpolar regions and high altitudes. This volume, *The Biology of Human Adaptability*, edited by Paul T. Baker and J.S. Weiner, was published by the Oxford University Press in 1966.

Secondly, there is the requirement of a *Guide*, or statement of the field activities needed to cope with the many problems put forward under the various research categories. To provide this guide, even in outline, is a formidable task and the material available to the Convener for doing this, is still incomplete. It is felt, however, that even a provisional and often sketchy treatment at this stage may still be of value to National Committees and teams planning their national activities for Phase II of IBP.

OUTLINE GUIDES TO FIELD WORK

GENETIC SURVEYS ON A
WORLD SCALE (CATEGORY 1A)

I   Scope and aims

In the attempt to achieve a comprehensive world genetical survey, three main stages are to be envisaged.

1   The compilation and circulation of existing published data, many of them in journals of small or local circulation, and ultimately the full statistical treatment of these data.

2   The collection, circulation and statistical treatment of unpublished data existing in the records of blood transfusion services and hospitals.

3   The performance of new surveys, with priority given to those needed to fill important gaps in the world record. Such surveys might range from

local investigations restricted to the ABO groups of a single population, to comprehensive investigations of several populations in a particular region, for a wide range of blood groups and other inherited factors. Thus any institution connected with blood grouping, however small, and however limited in resources, can make some contribution to the contemplated world survey. Similarly, even small expeditions, if well planned, could make valuable contributions towards the aim of obtaining genetic data on a world scale.

SOME SPECIFIC AIMS OF IBP SURVEYS

The distributional pattern of genetic characters has been used for a long time, like certain anthropological features, to elucidate the degree of relationship between populations on a local, regional, continental or world scale. To establish such relations on a secure basis a knowledge of a large range of genetic markers is necessary. The fact, for example, that much closer affinities exist between the Eskimo-Aleut stock and Asiatic Mongoloids than with their nearer neighbours, the American Indians, is based on the availability of data on the ABO, MN, Diego and other blood group data and by differences in the frequency of non-tasters, in the BAIB excretion rates, and the frequency of the haptoglobin types. It is also possible to state that Bushmen and Hottentots are closer to each other genetically than they are to Bantu-speaking Africans: they nevertheless have many characteristics in common with other Africans. Studies of affinity can be carried out to a high degree of discrimination, and these would be one desirable objective of intensive regional studies (under Category 2), but there is still much to be learnt on this question even from only general genetic surveys.

Another significant outcome of surveys is the uncovering of clines and gradients. The existence of these or of major discontinuities can only be substantiated and be made meaningful as more and more gaps between populations are filled in. The accretion of data has revealed the probable occurrence of a B-gene frequency cline extending from Central Asia into North American Eskimo populations, comparable to that extending westwards into Europe. In the New Guinea region there may be an altitudinal cline correlated with a decreasing G-6 PD deficiency. Scrutiny of the South Africa data reveals a gradient of increasing frequency of both A and B blood group genes (and a decrease in O) as the Bantu populations of the south eastern regions of South Africa are traced into the Cape province so indicating a region of gene flow between Bantu and Hottentot.

The distribution of particular genes in relation to certain geographical features or to climate may suggest the operation of some selective factor. We need many more survey data to provide as complete a geographical picture as possible of those genes with a presumed relation to malarial resistance or sensitivity. The work carried out in New Guinea represents a large step in this process of mapping. The past and present distribution of many other diseases, lethal in the reproductive period of life, are known; a more detailed regional mapping of various blood group genes could well point to the existence of a selective influence. The claim that the ABO system is related to the prevalence of gastric cancer will only obtain validification when regions outside Europe are brought into the comparison.

General surveys may confidently be expected to reveal the presence at high frequencies in certain communities of hitherto 'rare' genes or to the discovery of new allelic variations and their modes of inheritance.

What has been said above on the blood group systems is for the most part applicable to other genetic factors which should be included in surveys if personnel and finance permit. For example, the frequency of non-tasters to P.T.C. has relevance to the existence of goitrogenic areas, skin colour to the selective action of ultra-violet light, and it may be that colour blindness is particularly low in still-existing hunting communities. Clearly there are many gradients and clines and other significant types of distribution to be discovered for these and other genetic characteristics.

The general genetic survey is an essential first step in all multi-disciplinary studies, involving comparisons between two or more communities as some indication of genetic similarity or dissimilarity is always of significance in such studies, whatever their special purpose might be.

II Field work—list of activities

The basic and minimal work is that stated below under 'primary activities'; depending on resources 'additional activities' can be added to the programme. All procedures and techniques are described in detail in IBP Handbook No. 9: *Human Biology: a Guide to Field Methods.*

A PRIMARY ACTIVITIES

1 Collection of blood: preferably 15 ml., packed in cooled containers and despatched for testing. At least 100 unrelated individuals should be in the sample.

2 Recording of personal, family and social data of all individuals from whom blood (and other genetic material) was collected. It is essential to be able to ascertain the family relationships between the individuals.

B ADDITIONAL ACTIVITIES

1 Recording of medical and nutritional data.
2 Collection of saliva: Saliva to be collected, boiled, stored and transported at low temperatures for subsequent testing. 100 specimens at least.
3 Collection of urine: Urine to be collected, preserved and transported for subsequent analysis of amino-acids. 100 specimens at least.
4 Testing for enzyme G-6 PD deficiency in the field.
5 Testing for taste blindness to P.T.C.
6 Dermatoglyphics: digital and palmar prints.
7 Skin pigmentation by spectrophotometer.
8 Colour vision by Ishihara charts, or preferably by anomaloscope.
9 Collection of hair samples for colour determination in the laboratory by spectrophotometry; and for determination of hair form.
10 Determination of eye colour using standard reference set.
11 Anthroposcopic characters of general interest, in particular eye form, ear form, nose shape and body hair distribution.
12 Dental characters of genetic interest.

C SPECIALIZED ACTIVITIES

1 Cytogenetic studies:
a buccal smears for sex-chromatin,
b cells cultured from skin biopsies.
2 Acetylation types: (urine tests following dose of sulphamethazine).

GROWTH AND PHYSIQUE SURVEYS ON A WORLD SCALE (CATEGORY 1B)

I Scope and aims

Human populations differ greatly in the range of body build, or physique, presented by their members. Some groups like the Dinka or Tutsi are tall and slender, others like the Apache are short and broad; some heavily muscled, others lightly so; some have short legs and long trunks, others the reverse. Correspondingly, the manner of growth of the children in these populations differs, for adult physique is a product of the growth process. There is much variation in physical characters within all populations, as well as between them, so that there is some overlap in the distribution of most measurements between most populations. But this does not obscure the large population differences observed in the average values.

The first aim of the IBP project on growth and physique is to reveal more clearly the extent of the population differences at present existing in the world, and to throw light upon the processes, genetic and environmental, which are responsible for them.

The physiques of individuals in a population depend on the distribution in the population of numerous genes and on the inter-action of the products of these genes with the environment during the whole period of growth and development.

Genetic differences have come about by natural selection; we must suppose that in each of the major populations of the world the growth of its members was gradually adjusted, by selection, to the environmental conditions in which they evolved. The remnants of this process we should be able to see in modern populations; the remnants only, because migrations have altered the distributions of peoples so that many no longer live in the areas in which they evolved.

These genetic differences are obscured, magnified or distorted, however, by the environmental circumstances, during growth, and in particular by nutrition and pathology. The growth of children is one of the best indices of child health that we possess, and a continuous monitoring of the growth and development of children should be a major concern of all governments in under- and over-nourished countries. A second aim of the growth and physique project is therefore to relate growth to the nutritional and other circumstances of children in a variety of countries, and to lay the foundation for a series of studies of growth at regular intervals, particularly in emergent countries. From both the biological and the medico-social points of view, it is important to make comparisons not only between different populations but between groups in the same populations living under differing social, nutritional, medical and climatic conditions. In this way we can find out to what extent present environments fall short of supplying those stimuli and substrates which are necessary if all members of the population are to fulfil the potentialities of their gene complex.

There have been in the past many anthropometric descriptions of adults and a few of children, the latter mostly in Western countries. But although the anthropologists of the past collected large amounts of data, often with admirable accuracy and standardization of techniques, they did so with the avowed aim of making racial or taxonomic comparisons. Their outlook was very different from that of the modern biologist, and their data tend to shed light on questions we now regard as irrelevant, while leaving totally in the dark the great questions of adaptation, selection, starvation and disease. Undue weight was given to cranial and facial measurements, and little or no attempt was made to assess the degree of muscularity or fatness. The older material is very deficient in measurements bearing on work capacity, nutritional status or growth patterns.

Existing data are also very unevenly distributed over geographical regions. We are totally ignorant of the build and growth of people in many areas of the world, for example in South West Asia outside Turkey and Israel. Nevertheless such information we have suggests that important ecological generalizations such as the Bergmann and Allen 'rules' may, within limits, apply to man. It seems likely, also, from the existing fragmentary data, that differences in growth rates and age of puberty follow both genetic and climatic clines. But much more information is required before we can accept or reject such generalizations. Amongst Negro peoples north of the Equator, for example, there are data on the stature of adults in about 200 populations. But in only 4% of these is there information about other factors which are of much more importance for adaptation. And for children's growth there are no data at all. The fact is that the growth characteristics of almost every population except the European and North American are so little known that the study of any other group which is properly carried out would have real scientific value.

II Field work—list of activities

The activities required in carrying out this programme are given below; the details of the methods will be given in the Handbook. Meanwhile some methodological information can be supplied through the consultants mentioned below (p. 57).

A PRIMARY ACTIVITIES

1 Sampling of population. Where possible two or more contrasting samples of children of all ages and of adults should be drawn in each country or region, representing the well-nourished and ill-nourished, parasitized and non-parasitized, high-altitude and low-altitude, or

heavy-working and light-working sections of the population. Sampling may be of whole village communities; of whole school communities, or of district communities in urban areas. The method of choosing the sample will vary from one country to another; but whatever its nature the sample must be carefully defined and not haphazard.

2 Ascertainment of age. Amongst children great efforts will need to be made to ascertain correct ages, if necessary by reference to historical events.

3 Ascertainment of medical, nutritional and social circumstances. Some forms of medical examination (e.g. for parasite ova) will be impracticable for all individuals measured, but a sample of the population measured should, preferably, be examined at a similar time. Failing this, the sample to be measured should be selected from a group about whom previous medical surveys have established the basic facts.

4 Ascertainment of background, daily work activities and environmental conditions such as climate.

5 Anthropometric examination. The Handbook divides measurements into primary and secondary lists. The primary list consists of 31 measurements (including skinfolds) and the secondary list, to be done if time permits, a further 7. The measurements do not take more than a few minutes per subject; it seems likely, particularly in some countries, that collecting the subjects will occupy more time than measuring them.

6 Anthroposcopic examination. Particular attention should be paid to ratings of sexual development in children.

7 Dental examination: eruption and other data.

8 Menarcheal age inquiry. Listed separately because large scale surveys can be very simply made of menarcheal age alone, without anthropometry. Simply record age and ask whether menstruation has begun or not.

B ADDITIONAL ACTIVITIES

These should be done where circumstances permit.

1 X-ray of hand and wrist for skeletal age determination.

2 Radiographic measurement of bone, muscle and fat in calf, upper arm and thigh in children and adults.

3 Standardized photography of whole body and of face.

C SPECIALIZED ACTIVITIES

1 Determination of bone density by wedge techniques.
2 Measurements of body volume and density by underwater weighing.
3 Determinations of body fluid spaces.
4 Determination of total body potassium by K^{40}

ADAPTATION TO HIGH ALTITUDES (CATEGORY 2)

I Scope and aims

The study of the adaptation and fitness of settled communities at high altitudes is one of the most important aims of the HAP. In mountainous regions one finds in comparatively small areas striking contrasts in atmospheric pressure, temperature, and terrain with ramifying effects upon nutritional and disease ecology. The object of the programme is to make an integrated study of the detailed interrelationships between the various ways in which man adapts to the totality of the variations in this type of environment. The areas suggested for study are the Andes, Himalayas, Ethiopian Highlands and the Caucasus.

Till now the Andes, particularly of Peru, have been the scene of the most active work on settled communities, while in the Himalayas the effect of extremely high altitude on reactions of non-indigenous groups (European) has been intensively pursued. Under HAP it is hoped that a better understanding of settled communities in different parts of the Andes (Chile and Bolivia, as well as Peru), the Himalayas, and the less well-known areas such as Ethiopia and the Caucasus will be the object of multinational team work.

It is at once clear that the complexity of the ecological situation makes it desirable that attempts should be made to use a research design based on 'interhabitat' and 'interpopulation' comparisons, as well as on adequate age-groups and family linked subjects in order to distinguish between genetic and non-genetic components in adaptation. A discussion of these design problems will be found in papers by Harrison, Baker and Schull in *The Biology of Human Adaptability*. A simplified scheme is given below.

A secondary objective of high altitude studies is the study of the responses of indigenous peoples to altitudes higher than those normally inhabited, i.e. over 18,000 ft., for comparison with results already obtained on Europeans.

II Outline scheme for high altitude study

1 Design of study The design of the study is essentially one of a comparison between two populations, one of which (A) has resided at high altitudes for a considerable number of generations [A(H)], but of which some elements have migrated to lower levels [A(L)]. The other population (B) has resided at low altitudes for many generations [B(L)], but has elements at high altitudes [B(H)].

Thus we have:

Population	Population
A(H)	B(L)
A(L)	B(H)

Comparisons can be made as follows:

1 A(H) and B(H)   Unique similarities are immediate phenotypic adap-
   A(L) and B(L)   tations. Differences are due to different ancestral origins.

2 A(H) and A(L)   Similarities are genetic and due to common ancestry.
   B(H) and B(L)   Differences are phenotypic adaptations.

3 A(H) and B(L)   Similarities are due to common factors in the four
   B(H) and A(L)   populations. Differences may be either phenotypic or genetic.

To identify the various groups may well be the object of pilot expeditions. The main objectives of such expeditions would be:

a Determination of the population structure in the region, both ethnically and in relation to altitude.

b Establishing good relations with the inhabitants so that subsequent larger parties would meet with a reasonable degree of co-operation. To achieve this end, pilot expeditions would have to practise a good deal of clinical medicine.

4 The samples As far as possible, unrelated subjects should be studied. Two separate methods of sampling should be used.

a   Unrelated adults.
b   An age dependent sample (to detect any differential selection as well as environmental modification). It would be useful but not absolutely essential for the size of this sample to be based on the age structure of the population.

Adults   c. 200 in each of the 4 groups
            [A (H), A (L), B (H), B (L)]

Age dependent 0–3
            4–10   } c. 200 per group
            11–17

A group of 0–1 should also be included if feasible, i.e. 800 (1000) per group, 3200 (4000) *in toto*

3   Field work—list of activities

A   PRIMARY ACTIVITIES

1   *Background information*
a   Medical examination of all individuals along the lines suggested in *HA* 26/2.
b   Demographic information: This would follow the lines laid down in *HA* 25. Particular attention would be paid to: (i) pregnancy histories, mortality figures; (ii) social factors affecting fertility.
c   Basic nutritional survey.
d   Blood would be taken for sero-genetics and for the following special medical examinations: (i) bacterial and viral antibodies; (ii) blood parasites; (iii) haemoglobin concentration, MCV, PCV, MCHC; (iv) plasma proteins, plasma lipids, creatinine; Vitamin A and carotene.

2   *Genetic studies*
a   Blood: 15 ml. of blood to be collected and packed in cool containers and despatched for testing. Tests would always be made for: (i) blood group antigens (always: *ABO*, A_1, A_2, BH; MNSs; *P*, P_1; *Rh* C D D^u E c e; *Kell*, K; *Lewis*, Le^a Le^b; *Duffy* Fy^a; *Diego*, Di^a); (ii) haemoglobins; (iii) serum proteins (always: haptoglobins and transferrins).
b   Urine to be collected for urinary amino-acids (always: BAIB).
c   Saliva to be collected, boiled and transported at low temperatures (tested always for secretor status).

d   Other genetic studies: a full list is given in *HA* 23. Observations would comprise: (i) colour blindness; (ii) taste blindness; (iii) dermatoglyphics; (iv) pigmentation of skin by spectrophotometer and of hair and eyes by reference sets; (v) anthroposcopic observations including eye folds, eye shape, body hair, lip form, nose shape, nail form); (vi) dental characteristics.

3   *Physiological studies, including fitness and working capacity*
a   Respiratory capacity and related observations. Observations would include: (i) forced expiratory volume; (ii) forced vital capacity; (iii) breath-holding time; (iv) chest expansion; (v) chest X-ray.
b   Working capacity and related observations. Observations would always include: (i) assessment of maximal O_2 uptake; (ii) sub-maximal work test; (iii) resting heart rate and blood pressure (part of medical examination); (iv) a test of muscular strength.

4   *General population characteristics*
a   Anthropometry: desirable measurements in relation to respiratory function, working capacity, temperature tolerance, growth and genetic constitution.
b   Standard close-up photography.

B   ADDITIONAL ACTIVITIES
These should be done according to resources, trained personnel and equipment.

1   *Nutritional studies*
a   to determine calorie, protein and mineral intake.
b   assessment of background 'habitual activity'.

2   *Physiological studies*
a   Tests of cold tolerance—whole body;
b   tests of cold tolerance—peripheral;
c   tests of heat tolerance;
d   comfort zone determinations;
e   tests of thermal pain;
f   tests of thyroid function;
g   samples collected for adreno-corticoids;
h   tests of skilled performance (vigilance, etc.).

3 *Physique and growth*
a X-ray of hand and wrist for skeletal age determination;
b radiographic measurement of bone, muscle and fat in calf, upper arm and thigh in children and adults;
c standardized photography of whole body, and of face.

4 *Genetic studies*
Medical examination for congenital abnormalities using check list.

SPECIALIZED ACTIVITIES
In addition to physiological tests laid down in A and B above, the following special observations would be made in a separate investigation on about 12 indigenous subjects, tested at their normal altitudes as well as at very high altitudes:
a ergometer exercise at four work rates, with measurement of heart rate, ventilation and oxygen consumption to steady state. Also maximum work oxygen intake, heart rate and ventilation, and oxygen intake in recovery;
b arterial blood samples (or venous samples from heated hand) with measurement of oxygen capacity, oxygen and carbon dioxide content and pH, if possible in rest and exercise. Electrolytes on stored plasma samples;
c maximum pulmonary diffusing capacity;
d respiratory regulation, by the Lloyd-Cunningham technique;
e nutritional balance studies, 24-hr. energy balance.

THERMAL TOLERANCE (CATEGORY 2)

I Scope and aims
Our knowledge of immediate physiological responses to exposure of extremes of heat and cold is extensive. Much of this information has come from investigations in artificial climatic chambers but a substantial amount of confirmatory evidence has been obtained under more natural conditions. These studies have only been made on small numbers and a restricted range of subjects. There is a lack of real long term studies of indigenous peoples and insufficient attention has been paid to hereditary, as opposed to acquired characters. There is a great dearth of knowledge on females and age groups

other than young adult males. Thus the time is ripe for intensification of investigations on more representative population samples.

The assessment of adaptation and acclimatization to heat and cold has so far been carried out in rather scattered (and often hurried) studies of populations exposed to extreme climates. The IBP presents a unique opportunity for a rapid extension of our knowledge on a world-wide basis. In this way, a physiological distribution map of adaptation to climate could be obtained. Already patterns of response not anticipated from purely laboratory studies are emerging and it is to be expected that much more will be learnt of the mechanisms of adaptive processes in the heat regulatory, circulatory and other bodily systems. It is clear from the studies of the last 10 years or so that some surprising variations in adaptive responses to heat of different ethnic groups have been reported. How far this is related to physical type, genetic difference, fitness, growth in a hot environment or even to the test conditions remains to be clarified. It is of great interest to determine the extent of natural, physiologically acquired adaptation as compared to genetically determined responses in particular populations, which may be reflected in bodily size and physique, skin colour, etc. Simple ethnic groups are of particular importance here. Finally, a knowledge of the limits of adaptation and the causes of breakdown and loss of acclimatization has a direct bearing on standards which need to be laid down for mental and physical work, sleep and for optimum growth and development. A knowledge of such limits is obviously of practical value at a time of increasing numbers in the human populations with an increased rate of improvement in communications.

It is astounding to realise how many populations there are about which virtually nothing is known, e.g. the ecological adaptations of the peoples in the Congo, Amazonian, Indian and S.E. Asian regions have not as yet been explored in terms of either physiological, genetic or cultural responses. For communities of arid or semi-arid regions such as the Australian aborigines, South African Bushmen or the Bedouin some data have been obtained but our knowledge remains very scanty and superficial.

Many investigations appropriate to IBP urgently require to be undertaken and naturally only a few of these can be mentioned here, but in all of them the value of standardized methods in order to make valid comparisons is evident e.g. the studies of cold tolerance should be extended to an examination of newly arrived migrants, of Negroes in Europe, Italians in Australia; of subsequent generations, including hybrids, of various ethnic groups which have recently adopted a westernized culture; of particular occupations, e.g., fishermen, lumberjacks.

As regards tolerance to heat, other topics of interest include short-term acclimatization and de-acclimatization in migrants, e.g., Australian Queensland sugar-cane workers, African industrial workers.

Other research projects on a world scale include:

Survey of skin colour of tanned or untanned skin in relation to incidence of ultra-violet light. Spectrophotometric assessment of skin colour should be used.

Survey of hot and cold industries in order to define the range of comfort zones for efficient working and housing. The comfort limits would take into account the amount of clothing worn, bursts of activity, dietary pattern, time spent out of doors, age and sex.

The relation between body build and climate postulated on the 'Bergmann and Allen Rules' requires extensive confirmation, with more exact assessment of physique and body composition and climatic variables.

Information on salt requirements and water and salt metabolism including endocrine adjustments (ADH, aldosterone) remains meagre.

II Field work—list of activities

A PRIMARY ACTIVITIES

1 *Background observations*
a Medical observations of all individuals;
b Demographic information for subsequent sampling;
c Basic nutritional assessment;
d Collection of blood for basic genetic characterization;
e Assessment of habitual activity of subjects;
f Anthropometry—desirable measurements in relation to heat and cold tolerance, working capacity, physique: these comprise as essential measurements:
  i skinfold thickness at 10 sites,
  ii height and weight,
  iii surface area measurements,
  iv span,
  v chest, girth and width,
  vi arm and leg circumferences;
g Work capacity assessment (q.v.).

2   *Cold tolerance*

a   Whole body cooling either by eight-hour trial exposure test or by day trial test or both. In both tests the basic measurements should *always* include:

  i   skin temperatures at the agreed ten sites to give average skin temperature;
  ii   toe and finger temperatures, to give information of peripheral blood flow;
  iii   as 'core' measurements the rectal temperature always;
  iv   oxygen consumption by continuous sampling;
  v   shivering by EMG;
  vi   EEG for overnight sleeping tests;
  vii   urine output.

Environment. Both tests should be carried out in standardized mobile cold rooms so that various sources of error (as well as inconvenience) in past tests would be eliminated.

The environmental conditions in cold and control rooms should be specified in terms of:

  i   dry and wet bulb temperature by ventilated psychrometer;
  ii   black globe temperatures (an *optional* additional method is to measure mean radiant temperature by radiometer);
  iii   air movement by kata and by an orifice anemometer (additional *option*: hot wire anemometer).

The micro-environmental temperature should always be specified.

b   Cold induced vasodilation test using the finger.

c   Cold pressor test.

3   *Heat tolerance*

a   The basis of a heat tolerance test should remain a hot room test; that two standardized conditions should be used ('hot dry' and 'hot moist') with two levels of work (continuous) for three hours; with a pre-test equilibrating time of one hour; the subject prehydrated and allowed a fixed amount of water every hour during the test; work to be adjusted for differing age groups and females. The environmental conditions in the hot room should be specified in a standardized manner in terms of dry and wet bulb temperature by ventilated psychrometer, radiant temperature by black globe thermometer (optional addition by radiometer), air movement by Kata and an orifice anemometer (optional addition by hot wire anemometer).

b   The basic observations should always include:

 i as 'core' temperature the rectal temperature *always*; the ear temperature was strongly recommended as an additional optional method;

 ii skin temperatures;

 iii sweat loss to be determined; drip and water in shorts to be estimated;

 iv the heart rate to be determined by ECG;

 v oxygen cost of the work for every individual day of the test should be determined;

 vi record of urine output to be kept.

c   For heat tolerance test ancillary observations should include:

 i skinfold thickness at 10 agreed sites,

 ii height and weight;

 iii surface area measurements;

 iv outdoor conditions.

4   *General climatic characteristics*

a   Comfort zone determinations.

B   ADDITIONAL ACTIVITIES

1   *Cold tolerance*

a   calorimetric determination of finger blood flow during standardized cold exposure;

b   hand blood circulation by plethysmography during local cold exposure.

2   *Heat tolerance*

a   Sweat collection: during test an arm bag for sweat collection is permissible, the area covered to be rigidly specified; concentration and total content of electrolytes to be determined at specified intervals;

b   Plethysmography by strain gauge where equipment is available.

3   *General climatic characteristics*

a   Estimations of salt intake require a careful survey method of daily food and water intake combined with determination of 24-hr. urinary loss.

Ancillary information includes specification of environmental conditions and activity of subjects;

b   Where 24 hr. urine samples can be collected satisfactorily, preserved and despatched to a suitable laboratory, consideration should be given to determinations of:

  i   ADH in the sample;
  ii   Aldosterone in the sample;
  iii Na and K levels;
  iv   17 Ketosteroids.

C   SPECIAL ACTIVITIES

1   The V-test for 2 point discrimination in the cold is in practice a difficult test requiring a high degree of co-operation and in its present form unsuitable. Tests of performance such as manual dexterity are desirable and promising but require special attention by particular investigators.
2   Tests of thyroid activity during cold and heat exposure.
3   Enumeration of sweat glands—total count and distribution using a standardized procedure.
4   Tests of thermal pain by dolorimeter.

WORKING CAPACITY OF SELECTED POPULATIONS (FROM HA 50) (CATEGORY 3A)

I   Scope and aims

The morphology and physiology underlying work capacity and exercise fitness are variable characteristics and are at least to some extent subject to improvement or reduction through all phases of life. The capacity to change the functional dimensions is difficult to assess except probably on those champion athletes who have trained their body to the limit of its adaptability. The level of functional fitness, however, can be measured with acceptable scientific techniques, while morphological aspects can be evaluated through determination of the shape and the composition of the body. The functional evaluation should be based upon measurements of the energy mechanisms. The aerobic and anaerobic muscle metabolism can be studied separately and the capacities assessed by an experimental physiological approach, applicable even under field conditions. The aerobic work capacity depends upon a proper functioning of the circulatory and respiratory systems, and reflects accurately the all-over functional capacities of certain organs. A great battery of reliable tests is available for evaluating functional aspects of the lungs and of the circulatory apparatus. Since external work is performed by the contraction of the muscles, regulated and co-ordinated by the nervous system, the functional adaptability of the neuro-muscular apparatus as a whole is an important part of an individual's work capacity. The complexity of the functional aspects connected to this system, makes an evaluation extremely difficult, and at present all that seems reasonable to recommend for IBP purposes are measurements of muscle strength under standardized isometric conditions.

Work capacity varies in relation to many factors: age, sex, training, state of nutrition, etc., which are documented in a few excellent studies bearing on the physiological aspects of this problem. While the results of the work hitherto undertaken undoubtedly have contributed to the understanding of many basic problems of the physiology and morphology of performance capacity, they are in general based upon measurements of so few subjects, that they do not characterize populations. Thus we do not know the range and variability of physical fitness of people in the societies of the world. We do not know the level of fitness required for and associated with successful living in the variety of patterns of life and cultures characteristic of the populations of today.

If a high degree of muscular skill, endurance and strength was a prerequisite for our ancestors' survival in hunting communities, it would be interesting to throw light upon this problem by investigating the fitness of peoples still living in subsistence economies. We might then find, as a result of natural selection, a noticeably higher level and a lower variance in fitness characteristics in primitive groups with a very different polymorphic range.

We can extend the range of fitness even further by looking at that part of the population which is most efficient from the physical point of view—the athletes who represent the upper end of the scale and compare them with the sedentary people of our urbanized societies. To delimit the state of fitness in this way would be a considerable achievement; it would serve as a frame of reference for the study of a wide diversity of occupations. With this background of knowledge it should be possible to discover how differences of fitness are brought about. For example, differences in daily pattern of activity, in the state of nutrition or climate may be associated with quite different effects on muscle function, in the capacities of the metabolic mechanisms and in morphological and functional aspects of the cardio-respiratory system.

It may be that the shape and the composition of the human body exerts a limitation on the extent and nature of the capabilities for fitness adaptability. The effect of the genetic element in producing differences in fitness may perhaps be considered by a study of athletes and their close blood relations.

In making comparisons between populations in terms of climatic adaptation, whether it be to tropical heat, desert conditions, cold or altitude, the state of physical fitness must be taken into account. Physical fitness has direct bearing on tolerance to cold, because high fitness is associated with increased capacity to produce heat by muscular activity. The few investigations into this subject suggest that physical fitness plays an important part in other aspects of tolerance to cold. There exists also some evidence which suggests that physically fit people exhibit greater working ability in the heat than the unfit.

The pulmonary functions which underlie working capacity, are influenced by the atmospheric pollution to which the subject is exposed; this may be local and specific to the subject, for example, smoking a cigarette or living in an igloo, or general as a result of industrial pollution of the atmosphere. The outcome may be a pathological condition. There are many more problems linked to the relation between fitness and pathology. For example, some evidence suggests that better fitness tends to reduce or delay the fatal consequences of degeneration diseases in the circulatory organs. These diseases also tend to reduce fitness. All aspects of this are far from well established. Whenever the fitness of a population is examined, the opportunity should be taken to relate this to medical and nutritional states of the subjects.

Systematic studies of populations in many different kinds of habitat, occupation, pattern of cultural and social living may be regarded as falling into the category of world-wide surveys planned for the Human Adaptability Project. But the study of fitness as defined for the purpose of the project is technically an exacting matter and not to be undertaken except by well equipped and well trained personnel. Fitness studies will become of greater significance when related to particular biological and ecological factors. This requires considerable ancillary information as well as careful sampling. It will be necessary, for any population, to have data on medical and nutritional background, the daily pattern of occupational and leisure time activity, the cultural and social life and status and the physique of the subjects.

II Field work—list of activities

1 Measurement of aerobic work capacity estimated from simple exercise tests.
2 Measurements of selected aspects of lung functions (forced expiratory volume).
3 Muscle strength, including measurements of isometric strength in the muscles of
a the underarm (handgrip);
b the upper extremities and shoulder girth;
c the torso;
d the legs.
4 Anthropometry—height, weight, skin fold measurements.
5 Medical examination of subjects prior to tests.
   Four classes of subjects are of major interest:
a School children of all societies;
b Adults of industrialized and urbanized communities, representing all occupations;
c People of simple communities where muscular activity is essential for survival;
d The athletic population of the world.

B ADDITIONAL ACTIVITIES
1 Measurement of maximal oxygen uptake by the direct methods and evaluation of related respiratory and circulatory measurements (pulmonary ventilation and heart rate in relation to oxygen uptake).
2 Pulmonary diffusion—capacity and airway resistance.
3 Assessment of habitual physical activity (O_2-uptake measurements, continuous heart rate recordings, calorie consumption based on nutritional surveys).
4 Photographic anthropometry.

C SPECIALIZED ACTIVITIES
1 Measurement of the capacity of the anaerobic muscle metabolism (maximal exercise blood lactate).

2 Determination of oxygen usage at which anaerobic metabolism occurs.
3 Measurements of body fluids (blood volume and total amount of haemoglobin).
4 Measurement of the size of the heart (by X-ray technique).
5 Measurement of cardiac output and arterial blood pressure during graded exercise loads.
6 Miscellaneous (for example measurements of indices of climate and altitude tolerance).

The additional and specialized activities require well equipped and highly trained research teams. They can not be carried out therefore on a widespread scale, and are therefore only suitable and recommendable for use in intensive studies.

DISEASE AS A SELECTIVE AGENT (CATEGORY 3B)

I Scope and aims

It has been postulated (Haldane) that infectious disease might well have been the most effective agent of natural selection of man in favouring the survival and reproduction of those individuals possessing genes making for resistance. Most chronic or degenerative diseases (e.g. arteriosclerosis) would not be expected to act as selective agents as they kill after reproduction has ceased, unless they are in some way also associated with decreased fertility. That genetic resistance to infectious (and some other) diseases exists is not in doubt, though in only a few cases, so far, has the responsible gene (and its metabolic role in disease protection) been identified.

This complex subject of genetic differences in susceptibility to disease, infectious and non-infectious, and in determining the manifestation and severity of disease can only be briefly mentioned here; the reader is referred to *Genetics and the Epidemiology of Chronic Disease*, U.S. Public Health Serv., Public. No. 1163, 1965, and to the report of the CIBA meeting HA 57). It is important however to emphasize the many urgent opportunities that exist for field research and that such work, although complicated to organize, falls appropriately within the scope of the Human Adaptability Programme, since multinational co-operation by interdisciplinary teams of human biologists would be needed. The following comments extracted from the report on the CIBA meeting give some idea of the opportunities and limitations:

Twin comparisons have been widely used but there is some difference of opinion as to their value. Satisfactory twin material is difficult to obtain and it is open to doubt how far results on twins are applicable to people in general. Although twin studies indicate that genetical factors are involved in resistance to some diseases it is difficult to press the analysis any further.

Some work has been done on the incidence of certain transmissible diseases in families. In this approach the disease is treated as a character for study by standard methods of mendelian analysis.

Another method is to collect a sample of patients suffering from some disease and to compare their phenotypes with those of an unaffected control population. Thus we can try to discover whether people who are blue-eyed or tall or have sickle-cell trait or the blood group-A antigen are more likely to get a particular disease than other people.

The incidence of malarial parasites in the blood of sickler or non-sickler children provides evidence that this trait confers protection against the disease. Studies have also been made on the ABO blood group frequencies of small-pox cases, of children with infantile diarrhoea and of R.A.F. personnel shown serologically to have been infected with influenza A_2 virus and interesting divergencies from control frequencies have been shown.

Some workers feel that the severity of the disease rather than simple case incidence is a better parameter to study. At least in severe epidemics, it is argued, attack rates are so high as to leave little room for genetical differences in susceptibility to be manifested. The response to very severe forms of a disease, for example cerebral malaria, can give useful information.

A number of cautionary comments can be made about this approach.

It may require very large samples to show a statistically valid effect. Unless there are good *a priori* grounds for suspecting an association between a given inherited character and a disease it may therefore be rash to embark on such a project. There are many pathogens and many genetical characters and a blind search for associations may be both fatiguing and futile.

In practice we may only be able to demonstrate rather *large* effects convincingly but quite small selective pressures may produce large changes if they are exerted for long enough. Also the selective pressures needed to maintain a polymorphism if the fitness of the abnormal homozygote is not greatly decreased (e.g. Hb^E, Hb^C) may be very small. This leads to the further point that premature mortality and reduction of fertility are the important parameters in natural selection. It is usually difficult to study mortality from a given disease directly either because modern therapeutic measures supervene or because other diseases introduce complications. We may have to infer effects on mortality from an assessment of severity. Fertility data is often laborious to collect and subject to inaccuracies.

It may be remarked that many infectious diseases, such as measles, are no longer an important cause of mortality in civilized countries, but they are worth studying because they were potent killers in the past, and still are in some parts of the worl. It is not always easy in this type of study to be sure that the control sample adequately represents the population from which the patients were drawn. Failure of design in this respect may blur the results or even lead to spurious conclusions.

Even if a statistically valid association is established it does not follow that there is a causal relationship. Other lines of evidence will have to be sought to strengthen this conclusion.

The method can be applied to either multifactorial or single-gene characters; by choosing suitable genes we can at least ensure clarity from the genetical standpoint. Ideally all genotypes should be directly identifiable but in practice this is not always possible. In studying multifactorial characters we are often uncertain how much of the phenotypic variability is due to environment and therefore irrelevant in the present context. Furthermore we cannot assume that phenotypically similar individuals are equally similar in genotype. Since disease susceptibility may depend not on the visible phenotype but on hidden effects of contributory genes, unsuspected heterogeneity of genotype may obscure the association under consideration.

In some studies the antibody to a given pathogen has been taken as the character to be examined in relation to genotype. Confusion may arise here because of close antigenic similarities between related but different pathogens. Close attention to the identification of the pathogen and to strain differences is desirable in all studies on the problem of resistance but it may involve much specialized laboratory work. It is an advantage to concentrate on pathogens which do not show excessive variability.

The titre of antibody is an unreliable index of inborn resistance since it may depend mainly on the frequency and dose of infection rather than on individual differences in capacity for response.

Another approach is to correlate the geographical distribution of a gene or phenotypic character with that of a particular disease. This method has yielded valuable information in the case of sickle-cell trait and G6PD-deficiency and it has been virtually the only method used to study the relation of thalassemia minor to malaria resistance. It seems likely that this approach will give the best results when a disease is holoendemic to a certain region.

The pitfalls of geographical mapping of a disease by serological methods were brought out at the CIBA meeting. Recent population movements may have disturbed geographical correlations; historical information on this point is desirable but by no means easy to obtain in some areas. Related methods are:

1 The study of gene frequency change in a population after eradication of a disease. If strong selective pressures are at work detectable changes might occur in a few generations. Very considerable labour, organization and optimism would be required to obtain clear results by this method. Population movements and also changes in public health which are apt to be associated with an eradication scheme would have to be taken into account.

2 The study of gene frequencies in populations which have moved to another region. Work of this kind has already been done on American and Caribbean populations derived from Africa. The two main complications which arise are the uncertainty as to the precise origins of the migrants and the need to make allowance for intermixture with other populations in their new home. In some regions which have attracted immigrants these mixtures are rather complex.

II Field work

Field work in this complex subject is very much a matter for the team concerned. In addition to the more general suggestion for research already mentioned the following specific topics presented at the CIBA meeting may be listed.

1 Comparison of controls and patients with infectious disease with respect to eye, blood group character and also hair colours;

2 Twin comparisons in non-European regions;

3 Genetical studies on the populations of regions, for example, an epidemic of yellow fever;

4 Genetical studies on populations into which certain viruses have not yet spread and again after these viruses reach them;

5 The study of blood groups in relation to infantile diarrhoea in under-developed countries with a high incidence of cases;

6 Investigation of African and American Negro resistance to vivax malaria.

It is clear from the experience of field workers that for successful results well-equipped and manned teams are essential, comprising geneticists, epidemiologists and specialists in the disease under study. To put a team of this kind into the field would in all but a few cases call for a multinational effort of the kind that the Human Adaptability Programme (particularly in association with WHO) is designed to stimulate. The ideal would be for several teams to be ready to go to the scene of an epidemic of an infectious disease and to carry out the clinical, pathological, demographic and genetic comparison of affected and non-affected individuals and families: from an investigation of this kind arose the claim that the ABO polymorphism was related to a differential susceptibility to smallpox.

For sustained and systematic enquiries the best opportunities appear to lie in arranging working associations between teams and units of geneticists and epidemiologists already working in this vast and medically highly important field. WHO is of course a major stimulatory agency for field research and sustains a large programme covering all the main communicable and non-communicable diseases. Of particular interest to population geneticists are the activities of WHO teams and units concerned with the diarrhoeal and enteric diseases including cholera, virus diseases such as the respiratory and arthropod borne yellow-fever and haemorrhagic fevers, and also measles and smallpox; in the parasitic category, in addition to those already mentioned, are trypanosomiasis, amoebiasis and ankylostomiasis.

Genetic work during major epidemics requires considerable planning and organization because local medical resources are usually strained to the limit in such epidemics, and unless workers trained to collect the relevant material are present little can be achieved. Not only must arrangements be made for collection and shipment of blood specimens in good condition but case records must be carefully collected for the assessment of severity. Studies on non-immune populations when an epidemic strikes might be of considerable interest. However such populations today are to be found only in very isolated areas in which work is difficult. They will generally be small populations so that the amount of material for statistical analysis will be restricted.

SOCIO-DEMOGRAPHIC FACTORS AFFECTING GENETIC STRUCTURE: POPULATION DYNAMICS (CATEGORY 3C AND 3D)

I Scope and aims

Social and demographic factors influence the genetic structure profoundly, generally, by acting as internal or external barriers to gene flow. Amongst human populations there exist groups ranging from virtually closed isolates of various sizes and with varying intensities of inbreeding to groups exposed to every degree of mixing with neighbouring or migrant communities. At this period of history we are witnessing the progressive disappearance of many long established isolated and inbreeding communities. It is obviously a matter of some urgency to utilize the special opportunities for genetic analysis provided by these communities before they are broken up for ever. This is one reason for a concerted and organized effort in the immediate future such as is planned in the IBP. Reasons for putting special stress on the study of primitive groups are manifold and are given in the WHO Technical Report (1964) on this subject. That multi-national resources are needed is clear from field work of expeditions such as those organized by Tobias in South Africa, Salzano in Brazil, Kirk in New Guinea and Skoryna in the Easter Islands.

The genetic structure of the isolates and of migrant populations forms the subject of the detailed symposium volume edited by Goldschmidt (1963). Some aspects can also be illustrated by reference to papers in the *Biology of Human Adaptability*. Schull presents in detail the requirements for field studies and discusses in particular problems of sampling in this volume.

The operation and consequences of socio-demographic factors can be traced in many cases in some detail. Consanguinity studies afford favourable opportunities. There is now quite a good deal of information on degrees of inbreeding for various communities though it is urgently necessary to obtain much more on primitive communities. For example, how far is it generally true for primitive hunting and gathering groups that there was, as Salzano and Neel state, 'a high degree of inbreeding, at least at certain times of their evolution'? Insufficient is known of the consequences of inbreeding or its relaxation in particular on fertility, growth and physique. If, in sufficient groups, analysis could be made of widely differing intensities of inbreeding this would throw much needed light on the operation of 'heterosis'. This in turn has a close bearing on the underlying causes of secular trends in size and development. The influence of matings of relatives of varying distance on height can be seen from a Japanese study (Schull). The study of new crosses needs to be carried beyond the first generation. Such a longitudinal approach it is hoped would be instituted through IPB.

In the primitive groups socio-sexual selection leading to differential fertility must often be operative. Neel and Salzano give an instance from their Xavante study in which a tribal chief through polygamy is responsible for the genetic endowment of nearly one third of the next generation. In New Guinea conditions for this to happen are also in evidence (Kirk). In the Angmags-salik isolate of East Greenland one man who had been married three times had over 100 persons connected to him as a common ancestor (Laughlin). The fertility differentials within groups have a clear bearing on the 'founder principle'. The endowment of a whole series of populations in a new environment may be predominantly determined by a very closely related family group. This has often been postulated and Salzano and Neel give an instance which shows how this process may begin. In Birdsell's view it is possible to argue that the entire Australian continent could have obtained its population from one small migrant group. Repeated observations in a given region with detailed recording of the genealogies is quite likely to reveal the operation of fertility differentials in simple subsistence groups.

The intermixing of previously separated groups provides opportunity not merely for validating various hybridization models but may well yield important contributions to human genetics. For example, Haldane suggests that through careful family studies involving such mixture it may be possible to uncover the existence of pleiotropic morphological effects on some of the marker genes. A longitudinal community study in Israel of the kind discussed by Edholm offers a chance of observing effects of this kind. The study of the dynamics and consequences of gene flow between contrasting populations is particularly urgent where representative communities of the parental stocks are still to be found. One basic issue is the need to establish measures of 'genetic distance' between population groups. An illustration is given by Sanghvi who has made a special study of caste barriers in India. Both Kirk and Schull refer to the difficulties of assessing affinity through descent when it is certain that the frequency of some of the genes is subject to fairly rapid change through selection.

Demographic data as such have hitherto not been as widely utilized in studies of the biology of non-western human populations as they deserve. This stems partly from the fact that demography has tended to be regarded as a social science, partly that biologists have not been fully aware of the wealth of the quantitative information that may be available for a human population, or how useful this can be in problems of human ecology, nutrition, genetics, epidemiology and health. In the postwar period however, a number of studies have demonstrated that such data of adequate reliability can be collected, and for example in genetics, have shown how they can be used to trace the action of natural selection and at what ages it is effective, to partition selection into components due to differential fertility and mortality, to show how changes in isolate size are being brought about and at what rates, and what their biological effects are, and more generally to test assumptions about genetical models.

The details given below indicate the type of information that it would be profitable to include in the studies of human population biology which are covered in the IBP. With the Programme's focus on the natural resources on which human life depends, it is obvious that demographic work should concentrate on the activities that facilitate or inhibit or regulate reproductive success or failure or wastage, and how they change with changing biological and social motivations.

A PRIMARY ACTIVITIES

II Field work

1 PERSONAL AND DEMOGRAPHIC DATA
These are required in relation to fertility and survival, population growth, inbreeding effects.

The detailed proforma (HA25/2) must be used carefully in obtaining and recording the data. The information *cannot* be obtained with any degree of accuracy from a primitive people by any short intensive system of interviewing. What is required is the long-period indirect method of the field anthropologist, highly trained both in the art of non-directive interviewing and in the concepts of theoretical anthropology and psychology. Ideally such an individual would precede the biological investigation team and probably largely complete his demographic investigations before their arrival; during this period he or she would become acquainted with the social system of the population, and with the finer linguistic points, identifying individuals in a genealogical matrix and, by residence and social position, map the villages relevant to the investigation, and obtain detailed knowledge of those cultural variants which may lead to inaccuracy or falsification of information specifically required in the programme. During this period he or she should learn which matters have to be handled with extreme tact, for many of the questions requiring answers are indeed likely to lead to potentially explosive situations either as regards the stability of relationships within the population studied or as regards the safety of the investigators themselves. It may well be that some of the questions cannot be answered by any one subject or in a given social situation, because of inability, unwillingness or prohibition to divulge the information; but if none of these restrictions apply then there is little reason why the required information should not be obtained by a properly trained competent investigator. Success will depend on the methods he uses; if an interpreter's services are used, the investigator will probably find it profitable to use a male interpreter when dealing with male subjects, and a female when talking to female subjects. The whole data should be collected by interviews with one subject at a time, not with a group, and the proforma has been designed with this object in view; checking comes from comparison with the personal observations of the investigator, and from comparison with the information given by other individuals; when discrepancies are obvious, then re-interview should on no account suggest that additional information has come from some other source. The apparent repetition in parts of the pro-forma is deliberate, designed to allow further clarification on the part of the interviewed; re-interview should cover more than the points in doubt, in order not to direct attention to these.

a *Identification data; ascertainment of age*
Part one of the proforma is devoted to identification of the subject and ideally should be completed for every individual in a community and certainly for all those on whom detailed biological studies will subsequently be made. Apart from its value for identification purposes and for establishing genealogies, from it will also emerge useful information on geographic dispersal of individuals and hence of gametes, on fertility and the utilization of the female reproductive span, and on mortality.

b *Developmental data*
Developmental history of each living offspring; individual peculiarities.

c *Marriage data*
This part of the proforma should be completed for all individuals. From it should emerge some idea of the importance of marriage as the threshold to reproduction in the community, the distribution of ages at which reproduction commences; this section is of primary importance in any subsequent study of fertility.

d   *Sexual activity and relations*
Attitudes to sexual activity in many primitive peoples are quite different from those in western peoples, but though this is known there is very little objective quantitative information available.

e   *Females: reproductive records; menarcheal age inquiry etc.*
Whereas the questions in the preceding sections of the proforma are to be completed with reference to subjects of both sexes during the investigation, the present section refers exclusively to females and aims to discover and as far as possible quantify knowledge and behaviour of women in respect of reproductive activities. No male investigator is likely to complete satisfactorily this part of the proforma but there is little reason why a properly qualified female field worker should not obtain adequate answers. There is practically a complete dearth of information on the subjects dealt with in this section in the literature relating to non-western peoples and there is little enough on western peoples.

2   SAMPLING OF POPULATIONS
As required by design of the study.

3   HEALTH STATISTICS (adults and offspring)
a   Medical history (*see* HA26/2);
b   Physical examination (*see* HA 26/2);
c   Congenital defects identified (*see* HA 26/1);
d   Basic nutritional assessment;
e   Blood and urine collections for medical purposes;
f   Dental examination.

4   GENETIC AND PHYSICAL DATA
a   Collection of blood, urine and saliva for genetic purposes (q.v.);
b   Anthropometric examination (q.v.);
c   Anthroposcopic examination;
d   Pigmentary and other observations of genetic importance (q.v.).

B   ADDITIONAL AND SPECIAL ACTIVITIES

1   Medical examination—X-ray examination; E.C.G. observations.
2   Cytogenetics.

3 Physique and Growth
a X-rays of hand and wrist for skeletal age determination;
b Radiographic observations of muscle, bone and fat;
c Standardized photography.
4 Performance and Physiological Tests
a Tests of physiological fitness—work capacity;
b Tests of respiratory function;
c Tests of skilled performance.

SPECIAL NUTRITIONAL PROBLEMS
(CATEGORIES 2 AND 3E)

I Scope and aims

In every study of populations, whether in relation to climatic extremes, contrasts in habitat, selective effects of disease, level of fitness, in fact as an inescapable aspect of human adaptability, account must be taken of the nutritional condition of the population. This underlines the difficulties of field study and the need for a multidisciplinary and intensive approach. The nutritional factor may be considered from two aspects, which are not easy to separate. There is first the routine requirement for some form of nutritional assessment of all individuals and groups participating in an investigation. This, as already remarked, is one of the aims of any multidisciplinary intensive study. The nutritional status is in the nature of essential background information.

The second aspect is to single out nutritional 'parameters' for particular study as IBP projects. The nutritional factor then becomes the primary aim. The field is of course vast and only a few very tentative suggestions, arising from views expressed at discussions on IBP, are made here.

1 CALORIE AND PROTEIN REQUIREMENTS
IN DIFFERENT HABITATS

If, under Category 3, regional studies are launched in a number of the localities singled out as specially suitable and urgent it should be possible to make an assessment of nutritional, particularly of calorie and protein intakes in a standardized way in a whole series of habits. FAO has urged the need for this to be done under IBP and WHO states that there is little factual information on protein intake for children and adolescents within the period 2–18 years.

It is perfectly clear that the calorie requirements ascertained in a whole series of habitats and populations will be related to several factors, notably differences in climate, in habitual activity, in available food sources, in average bodily size of the population. The information will be valuable for its own sake, as FAO insists, even if the exact reasons for differences in level may not be easily ascertainable. If, however, reliable assessments can be attached to the factors mentioned it may turn out that by using some relatively contrasting parameters the influence of the separate items might become apparent. This is an ambitious task but only to be attempted on an international scale.

From references made to nutritional requirements in the papers of the Burg Wartenstein volume it is clear that our knowledge of the calorie, protein and calcium intake of populations of differing activity patterns and in different climates is meagre. (It would be interesting, for example, to be able to compare peoples of the hot dry area of South West Asia with those of Northern Africa; or tropical peoples in South America, Africa and India and S.E. Asia.) Edholm records that only five gm of the protein of middle Eastern diets is of animal origin. Macpherson in a paper on New Guinea natives questions the present assumptions on protein requirements since it has been found that both men and women perform physical feats requiring great stamina on very low protein intakes. This comment draws attention to the need to relate level of work output in different populations to the very variable amounts of protein that we know are consumed. This question could be fruitfully studied in India judging from the data recorded by Malhotra which indicates large regional differences in protein consumption, for example in the Punjab compared to Madras, or Kerala. What the protein intake is of the mountain peoples subject to the physical stress of the terrain (as well as of cold) is not recorded, but these peoples, as described by Baker for the Andes and Pugh and Malhotra for the Himalayas, are capable of moving very large loads.

2   NUTRITIONAL CONTRASTS AND THEIR EFFECTS

Hiernaux and Tanner have drawn attention to some of the questions which arise when two groups subsisting on contrasting states of nutrition are compared. The contrast may be in terms of gross nutrition, that is between well-nourished and poorly nourished or semi-starving groups, or in terms of qualitative differences as in protein or fat consumption. The biological effects to be looked for would include: (i) the differences in physiological fitness measured as work capacity between the two groups; (ii) the changes in physique and growth that may have occurred (the birth weight and deposition of fat are of particular interest); (iii) fertility and family size, difficulties of labour, pelvic shape, appearance of puberty etc., are all of special importance. The enquiry could go further and compare the two populations in terms of their heat and cold tolerance and other physiological characteristics.

The significance of the biological effects would be greatly enhanced if it were possible to make similar comparisons on ethnically and genetically different peoples. It is quite likely that the genotype influences the expression of a nutritional defect. Thus the effect of low protein intake on groups in the Congo in Hiernaux's account would seem to be very different from the effects on Indian subjects mentioned by Malhotra. So far we have unfortunately very little information derived from analysis along those lines.

3   NUTRITION IN RELATION TO PREGNANCY AND
    INFANT DEVELOPMENT

Another question is whether the smaller sized shorter women in simpler communities are metabolically more efficient and suffer the disabilities of reproduction to a lesser degree than deprived females in the lower socio-economic classes of industrialized communities. Is it true that despite much lower protein and calorie intakes the birth rates are not adversely affected? It does seem to be the case that even women of poor physique and of general ill-nourishment in many developing countries appear to be able to sustain adequate lactations. A well based investigation would include a longitudinal study of weight gain of babies, under different conditions of nutrition in contrasting habitats (Category 2).

II   Field work

A   PRIMARY ACTIVITIES

1   *Background activities*
a   Basic demographic and personal data;
b   Basic medical and dental examination;
c   Collection of blood for medical and genetic purposes;
d   Basic anthropometry of physique and growth (q.v.);
e   Tests of working capacity;
f   Assessment of habitual activity;
g   Analysis of food intake frequency.

2 *Specific nutritional studies*
a Assessment of nutritional status—physical;
b Assessment of nutritional status—biochemical;
c Studies of calorie intake from food intake;
d Studies of protein intake from food intake;
e Salt and water balance (*see* 'Thermal Tolerance').

B ADDITIONAL ACTIVITIES

1 *Background activities*
a More advanced anthropometry; body composition;
b Further tests of working capacity.

2 *Nutritional studies*
a Protein intake by urine collection and analysis of urea and sulphate.

C SPECIAL ACTIVITIES
1 Results of feeding tests;
2 Introduction of new foods.

MEDICAL AND EPIDEMIOLOGICAL TOPICS (CATEGORY 4)

It is clear, from the topics outlined in previous sections, that the physiological and genetic study of small communities, of isolates or of samples of large populations will pose many questions of medical interest. It should be clear also that many medical studies could be readily superimposed on the types of investigations listed. As the field of medical research is so vast and the IBP is primarily concerned with basic biological research it would seem reasonable, in the programme under 'Human Adaptability', to admit those topics of medical interest which have a direct bearing on the problems listed and which (for example, in epidemiology) can readily be incorporated into the field research.

A number of proposals for specific medical or epidemiological surveys have been made which are quite compatible with the survey programmes given in Categories 1 and 3A. These particular proposals are in fact for the most part under active investigation under the auspices and guidance of WHO. The appropriate section of WHO should be consulted if it is desired to include such proposals in a national HA programme. The topics under this heading may be briefly outlined:

1 *Surveys of blood pressure* in relation to age, sex and occupation: If carefully controlled observations can be made on the many different populations coming under study in HAP, particularly more remote and isolated groups, it would form a valuable addition to data already being collected. Observations on blood pressure would have little value unless comprehensive population data were also being collected, particularly on medical nutritional status, habitual activity, working capacity and physique. In the intensive field studies of HAP this many-sided examination would be done along with collections of blood and other material. Thus, estimates of serum cholesterol and lipoprotein fractions would be made in relation to blood pressure determinations.

2 *Haematological data:* Surveys are already going on to collect information by standardized methods and as part of the multidisciplinary regional studies of Categories 1 and 2. Blood collections would yield information on haemoglobin and haematocrit value and blood counts. Such information is obviously important in establishing the prevalence of various anaemias, particularly iron deficiency anaemia (which in many areas is a major health problem). These surveys are relevant to the surveys of abnormal haemoglobins which in turn have important bearings on the relation of these genetic factors to disease susceptibility.

3 *Antibody surveys:* Blood collections during surveys and regional studies under HAP will greatly extend the range of populations on which information on disease antibodies is available. If carried out on a wide scale, such surveys, which clearly have value for public health, will yield information on the geographical distribution of a number of infectious agents.

4 *Certain blood constituents:* More information is needed on certain biochemical constituents in relation to age, sex, fitness, occupation and climate; in particular, the following:

a *Plasma proteins.* A better knowledge of serum proteins is urgently needed for an understanding of the metabolic alterations occurring in such conditions as protein malnutrition and disease in which protein breakdown is accelerated or in which there is protein loss.

b *Plasma lipids.* Estimates of serum cholesterol and lipoprotein fractions, among other substances in the blood, are of importance in community studies of atheriosclerosis.

c *Creatinine.* There is suggestive evidence that individuals living under conditions of dietary protein restriction have lower blood plasma levels of some non-protein nitrogen fractions.

d *Vitamin A.* Plasma vitamin A and carotene levels should be determined, as they could reveal deficiencies as yet unknown in some areas of the world and contribute to a better understanding of the epidemiology of vitamin A deficiency.

5 *Survey of congenital defects:* The few surveys so far made of congenital defects suggest that human populations may differ appreciably in their characteristic spectra of frequencies of different types of defect and it is possible that their total loads of defect also differ. In the type of field investigation in primitive populations envisaged under the IBP it would be of interest to obtain some indication of the numbers and types of defect that occur. It would not be possible, initially at any rate, to make a survey of all births over a period among these peoples as is at present being done under the auspices of the WHO among samples of more advanced populations. Moreover, many of the defects that cause only slight reduction in survival probability in Western populations may indeed be lethal in the more rigorous conditions under which primitive populations live. Whatever is seen, then, may give a minimal estimate of the true frequency of occurrence. Nonetheless, it is felt that observations of the more easily identifiable conditions in the field would be of interest, partly in order to obtain a preliminary estimate of their frequencies and partly to draw attention to those populations in need of more intensive investigation.

For HAP programmes there is available a suggested list of gross conditions which a qualified observer can easily identify in the field without too protracted an examination of the subject and without having to undergo special intensive courses of preliminary instruction, and which careful history taking will distinguish from similar acquired conditions. This list is based on the list that a number of authors have themselves used under field conditions without complicated apparatus or sophisticated clinical facilities. Used on the Tristan da Cunha population, it has yielded very valuable findings. Those investigators wishing to utilize a more comprehensive list of congenital defects are referred to the WHO revised international classification of congenital defects. However, it must be stressed that remote and isolated populations may well manifest genetic or congenital conditions that are very rare or unknown elsewhere, or atypical forms of known aberrations. Findings of most interest will therefore accrue from careful descriptions of any deviations from normality rather than checking down any list, no matter how exhaustive.

DOCUMENTS RELATING TO PHASE II

WEINER J.S. (1964) The biology of man in the IBP. *Current Anthropology*, **5**, 191.

WEINER, J.S. (1964). A progress report on the Human Adaptability Section of the IBP. *Current Anthropology*, **8**, 417.

BAKER, PAUL T. & WEINER, J.S. (eds.) (1966) *The Biology of Human Adaptability* (Proceedings of Burg Wartenstein H.A. symposium): physiological, genetic and anthropological papers on Africa, South America, India, Australia and New Guinea, S. West Asia, Circumpolar regions and High Altitudes. Contributors: P.T. Baker, O.G. Edholm, G.A. Harrison, J. Hiernaux, J.A. Hildes, R.L. Kirk, K. Lange Andersen, W.S. Laughlin, R.K. Macpherson, M.S. Malhotra, J.V. Neel, L.G.C.E. Pugh, F.M. Salzano, L.D. Sanghvi, W.J. Schull, J.M. Tanner, P.V. Tobias, C.H. Wyndham, J.S. Weiner. Oxford University Press.

Research on population genetics of primitive groups. *WHO Tech. Rep. Ser.*, No. 387, 1968.

The use of vital and health statistics for genetic and radiation studies. *United Nations and World Health Organization*. 1962.

U.N. Conference on the Application of Science and Technology for the benefit of the less-developed areas (Agenda item F.1.1.) 1962.

Biology of human reproduction. *WHO Tech. Rep. Ser., No.* 280, 1964.

Immunological and haematological surveys: reports of a study group. *WHO Tech. Rep. Ser.*, No. 181, 1959.

Multi-disciplinary studies on primitive populations in Latin America. (Prepared for the Third Meeting of the Pan-American Health Organization Advisory Committee on Medical Research, 1964).

Research needs in human and animal tropical biometeorology. In *Tropical Health*, NAS-NRC Publn. 996, 1962. Washington: National Academy of Sciences—National Research Council.

Research needs in tropical climatology. *UNESCO Symposium on Arid Zone Problems*, 1960.

GOLDSCHMIDT, E. (ed.) (1963) *The Genetics of Migrant and Isolate Populations*. Williams and Wilkins, Baltimore.

MALHOTRA M.S. (ed.) (1965) *Human Adaptability to Environments and Physical Fitness*. Proc. of a Symposium held in New Delhi, Sept. 1965. Defence Institute of Physiology & Allied Sciences, Madras, India.

YOSHIMURA H. & WEINER J.S. (eds.) (1966) *Human Adaptability and its Methodology*. Japan Society for the Promotion of Science.

Problems in Human Adaptability. IBP Warsaw Meeting 26th—30th April, 1965. *Materialy I Prace Antropologiczne*, No. 75. Polskiej Akademii Nauk, Zaklad Antropologii, Wroclaw, 1968.

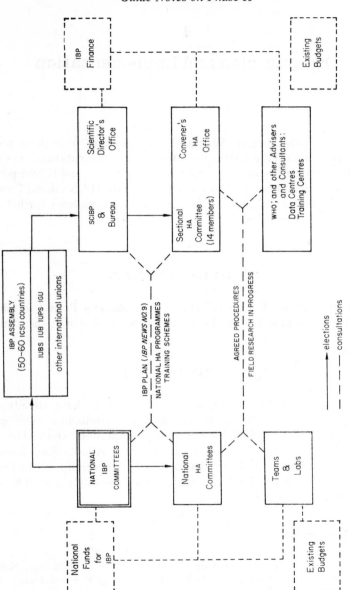

Functional relations between national bodies, international organs and officers of the Human Adaptability Project of IBP (1965), and sources of finance.

4

Organization and Implementation

The fulfilment of the Human Adaptability Programme, in both its phases, depends entirely on (1) the active and enthusiastic participation of teams and laboratories working through their National Committees and (2) the positive help and co-ordination provided by the SCIBP and the HA Sectional Committee. If these bodies play their part we can look with confidence for help also to WHO and other agencies.

A ORGANIZATION

The functional organization of the Human Adaptability Project in relation to the national and international bodies concerned is shown in the chart on p. 49.

1 NATIONAL LEVEL

The main national IBP Committees (of which over 30 have already been formed) contain human biologists (geneticists, physiologists, anthropologists, demographers or epidemiologists) for consultation on the HA programme. The appointment of National Human Adaptability Subcommittees is very important in order that national programmes can be formulated in detail. The following list gives the HA committees and HA correspondents as known at present.

Chairmen of HA committees

Country	*Name and Address*
Antarctica	Dr O.G. Edholm, Division of Human Physiology, National Institute for Medical Research (MRC Laboratories), Holly Hill, Hampstead, London, N.W.3, England

Country	Name and Address
Argentine	Professor Dr V.G. Foglia, Director, Instituto de Fisiologia, Consejo Nacional de Investigaciones Cientificas y Tecnicas, Rivadavia 1917, Buenos Aires, R. Argentina
Australia	Professor R.J. Walsh, School of Human Genetics, University of New South Wales, P.O. Box 1, Kensington, Sydney, New South Wales 2033
Austria	Dr E. Breitinger, Anthropologisches Institut, van-Swietengasse 7, Vienna IX
Belgium	Professor J. Hiernaux, Centre de Biologie Humaine, Institut de Sociologie, 44 avenue Jeanne, Brussels 5
Brazil	Dr F.M. Salzano, Instituto de Ciencias Naturais, Caixa Postal 1953, Porto Alegre, R.S., Brazil
Bulgaria	Professor D. Kadanov, Sofia 6, Boul. D. Blagoev 40
Canada	Dr J.S. Hart, Division of Biosciences, National Research Council, Ottawa
Chile	Dr R. Cruz-Coke, Division of Medicine, Department of Genetics, Universidad de Chile, Hospital Clinico Jose Jacquin Aguirre, Santiago 4
Congo	Dr J. Ghesquière, P.O. Box 194, Kinshasa XI
Czechoslovakia	Professor Dr O. Poupa, Institute of Physiology, Czechoslovak Academy of Sciences, Praha 4, Budejovicka 1083 (Sec. Docent Dr Med V. Seliger, Department of Physiology, Faculty of Physical Education and Sport, Ujezd 450, Praha 1, Mala Strana)
Finland	Professor H. Forsius, Head of Ophthalmological Department, University of Oulu, Uleaborg
France	Dr J. Sutter, Institut National d'Etudes Demographiques, 23—25 avenue Franklin D. Roosevelt, Paris VIIIe
Germany, Dem. Rep.	Professor J. Grimm, Institute of Anthropology, Humboldt-Universität 20, Berlin W8, Unter den Linden 6
Germany, Fed. Rep.	Professor Dr H. Walter, Am Fort Elizabeth 7, D-6500 Mainz.
Guatemala	Dr F.E. Viteri, Chief, Biomedical Division, Instituto de Nutricion de Centro America y Panama, Organization Mundial de la Salud, Carretera Roosevelt Zona 11
India	Dr L.D. Sanghvi, Human Variation Unit, Indian Cancer Research Centre, Parel, Bombay 12
Indonesia	Dr S. Prawirohardjo, Council for Sciences of Indonesia, Merkeda Selatan II pav., Djakata

Chapter 4

Country	*Name and Address*
Israel	Professor J. Magnes, Department of Physiology, Hebrew University, Hadassah Medical School, P.O. Box 1172, Jerusalem
Italy	Professor G. Montalenti, Istituto di Genetica dell' Universita di Roma, Citta University, Rome
Japan	Professor H. Yoshimura, Kyoto Prefectural University of Medicine, Hirokoji-Kawara-machi, Kamikyo-ku, Kyoto
Korea	Professor Yung Sun Kang, Department of Zoology, College of Liberal Arts and Science, Seoul National University, Seoul
The Netherlands	Professor Dr J.W. Tesch, Gesondheidsorganisatie TNO, Juliana van Stolberglaan 148, The Hague
New Zealand	Professor J.A.R. Miles, Department of Microbiology, University of Otago, P.O. Box 913, Dunedin
Nigeria	Dr A.E. Boyo, University of Lagos Medical School, Surulere, Private Mail Bag 12003, Lagos
Norway	Professor Dr K. Lange Andersen, State School of Physical Therapy, Trondheimsveien 132, Oslo 5
Philippines	Dr L.M. Sumabat, National Science Development Board, Port Area, Manila
Poland	Professor Dr A. Wänke, Polish Academy of Sciences, Institute of Anthropology, Wrocklaw, ul. Kuznicza 35
South Africa	D.J.M. Vorster, National Institute for Personnel Research, Council for Scientific and Industrial Research, P.O. Box 395, Pretoria
Spain	Professor E. Ortiz, Laboratorio de Genetica, Centro de Investigaciones Biologicas, Velasquez 144, Madrid 6
Sweden	Dr O. Wilson, Institute for Hygiene, Lund Universitet, Lund
Tanzania	Dr A.S. Msangi, Dar es Salaam School of Medicine, P.O. Box 20693, Dar es Salaam
Thailand	Professor O. Ketusinh, Department of Pharmacology, Faculty of Medicine, Siriraj Hospital, Bangkok
U.K.	Sir Lindor Brown C.B.E. M.B. F.R.S., Hertford College, Oxford
U.S.A.	Professor F. Sargent II, Dean, College of Environmental Sciences, The University of Wisconsin, Green Bay, Wisconsin
U.S.S.R.	Professor Z.I. Barbashova, Setchenov Institute of Evolutionary Physiology and Biochemistry, Academy of Sciences of the U.S.S.R., Leningrad K-223, Thorez Avenue 52
Venezuela	Professor M. Layrisse, Instituto Venezolano de Investigaciones Cientificas, Apartado 1827, Caracas
Yugoslavia	Professor V.P. Nikolic, Department of Experimental and Labour Physiology, Institute for Medical Research, Beograd

National HA correspondents

Country	Name and Address
Bolivia	Dr J.A. Vellard, Instituto Boliviano de Biologia de Altura, Edificio de la Faculdad de Medicina, La Paz
Burma	Dr Mya-Tu, Burma Medical Research Institute, No. 5 Zafar Shah Road, Rangoon
Colombia	Dr A. Restrepo, Facultad de Medicina, Apartado Postal 2038, Medellin
Ethiopia	Professor C.S. Leithead, Department of Medicine, Faculty of Medicine, Haile Selassie I University, P.O.Box 1176, Addis Ababa
Ghana	Professor Andoh, Department of Physiology, The University, Accra
Greece	Dr A. Poulianos, 73 E. Benaki Street, Athens 145
Hungary	Dr J. Nemeskeri, KSH Nepessegtudomanyi Kut, Csoport, Veres Palne ul. 10, Budapest V
Iran	Dr A. Shaybany, University of Teheran, Shahreza Avenue, Teheran
Kenya	Professor F.D. Schofield, Kenyatta National Hospital, P.O. Box 30588, Nairobi
Malaysia	Dr R. Bhagwan Singh, Institute for Medical Research, Jalan Pahang, Kuala Lumpur
Mexico	Dr S. Genoves, Institution de Investigaciones Historicas (Seccion de Antropologia), Faculdad de Ciencias, Planta Baja, Ciudad Universitaria, Mexico 20, D.F.
Mozambique	Dr D. da Costa Martins, Av. 24 de Julho 630–1°–1, Lourenco Marques
Peru	Professor M.T. Velasquez, Universidad Nacional Mayor de San Marcos, Faculdad de Medicina, Instituto de Biologia Andina, Apartado 5073, Lima
Roumania	Dr O. Necrasov, Corr. Member of Roumanian Academy, 8 Boulevard Dr Petru Groza, Bucharest
Switzerland	Dr P. Moeschler, Institute of Anthropology, rue Gustave-Revilliod 12, 1227 Carouge, Geneva
Tanzania	Dr A.S. Msangi, Dar-es-Salaam School of Medicine, P.O. Box 20693, Dar-es-Salaam
Uganda	Dr J. Bennett, Makerere University College Medical School, P.O. Box 2072, Kampala
Uruguay	Dr M.E. Drets, Casilla de Correo 1837 (Central), Montevideo

2   INTERNATIONAL LEVEL

IBP launched by ICSU is directed and supervised by SCIBP, which is elected by the periodic IBP General Assemblies consisting of representatives of all participating countries. The constitution of SCIBP is described in detail in *IBP News* No. 1. IBP has a permanent Scientific Director, Dr E.B. Worthington, at the Central Office at 7 Marylebone Road, London NW1. Of the present membership of SCIBP elected in July, 1964, those especially concerned with human biology are:

Prof. Montalenti (Vice President).

Prof. Weiner (Convener, Human Adaptability Project).

A Representative of the International Union of Physiological Sciences.

A Representative of the International Union of Nutritional Sciences.

The *Sectional Committee of Human Adaptability* is elected on as wide a geographical basis as possible with a balance between physiological and genetic interests. The Committee meets once a year and there are 10 full and corresponding members co-opted as required. The present members are as follows.

HA sectional committee

CONVENER

U.K.   Professor J.S. Weiner
                         c/o Royal Anthropological Institute
                         21 Bedford Square
                         London WC1

DEPUTY CONVENER

Belgium   Professor J. Hiernaux
                         Centre de Biologie Humaine
                         Institut de Sociologie
                         44 avenue Jeanne
                         Brussels 5

MEMBERS

U.S.S.R.   Professor Z.I. Barbashova
                         Setchenov Institute of Evolutionary Physiology and Bio-
                             chemistry
                         Academy of Sciences of the U.S.S.R.
                         Leningrad K-223
                         Thorez Avenue 52

Nigeria	Dr A.E. Boyo University of Lagos Medical School Surulere Private Mail Bag 12003 Lagos
Italy	Professor L.L. Cavalli-Sforza Institute di Genetica via S. Espifanio 14 Pavia
U.S.A.	Professor J.V. Neel Department of Human Genetics University of Michigan Medical School 1133 E. Catherine Street Ann Arbor Michigan
Brazil	Dr F.M. Salzano Institute de Ciencias Naturais Caixa Postal 1953 Porto Alegre, R.S.
South Africa	Professor P.V. Tobias University of Witwatersrand Medical School Hospital Street Johannesburg
Australia	Professor R.J. Walsh School of Human Genetics University of New South Wales P.O. Box 1 Kensington Sydney New South Wales 2033
Japan	Professor H. Yoshimura, Kyoto Prefectural University of Medicine Hirokoji-Kawara-machi Kamikyo-ku Kyoto

CORRESPONDING MEMBERS

U.S.A.	Professor P.T. Baker (Chairman, Multi-national high altitude studies) Department of Anthropology Pennsylvania State University University Park, Pa. 16802

Thailand	Professor O. Ketusinh Department of Pharmacology Faculty of Medicine Siriraj Hospital Bangkok
India	Dr M.S. Malhotra Director, Defence Institute of Physiology and Allied Sciences c/o Madras Medical College Madras 3
U.S.A.	Dr F.A. Milan (Chairman, Multi-national circumpolar project) Department of Anthropology University of Wisconsin Madison Wisconsin
Czechoslovakia	Professor O. Poupa Czechoslovak Academy of Sciences Institute of Physiology Praha 4 Budejovicka 1083
U.S.A.	Professor S. Robinson Indiana University Department of Physiology Bloomington Indiana
France	Dr J. Sutter Institut National d'Etudes Demographiques 23—25 avenue Franklin D. Roosevelt Paris VIIIe
Poland	Professor Dr A. Wänke Polish Academy of Sciences Institute of Anthropology Wroclaw ul. Kuznicza 35

At the Warsaw 1965 meeting the Sectional Committee decided that the informal system whereby the Convener has had technical help in drafting papers, etc., from a number of leading human biologists should be put on a more formal basis, and a number of honorary consultants have been appointed. They carried out the essential and onerous task of bringing together suggestions on methodology design and field work through correspondence and by organizing working parties. The honorary consultants, who would be glad to deal with queries, are at present as follows.

Honorary consultants

Growth and Physique Studies	Professor J.M. Tanner, Department of Growth and Development, Institute of Child Health, 30 Guildford Street, London, WC1, England
Blood Groups and Associated Surveys	Dr A.E. Mourant, Serological Population Genetics Laboratory, c/o St Bartholomew's Hospital, West Smithfield, London SE1, England
Studies on Genetic Structure of Populations	Professor J.V. Neel, Department of Human Genetics, University of Michigan Medical School, 1133 E. Catherine Street, Ann Arbor, Michigan, U.S.A.
Respiratory Physiology Studies	Dr J.E. Cotes, Pneumoconiosis Research Unit, Llandough Hospital, Penarth, Glamorgan, Wales
Work Capacity Studies	Professor K. Lange-Andersen, State School of Physical Therapy, Trondheimsveien 132, Oslo, Norway
Cold Tolerance Studies	Professor L.D. Carlson, School of Medicine, University of California at Davis, Davis, California 95616, U.S.A.
Heat Tolerance Studies	Dr C.H. Wyndham, Human Sciences Laboratory, Chamber of Mines Research Laboratories, P.O. Box 809, Johannesburg, South Africa
Heat Tolerance Studies (Controlled Hyperthermia Technique)	Dr R.H. Fox, Division of Human Physiology, National Institute for Medical Research (MRC Laboratories), Holly Hill, Hampstead, London NW3, England
Studies on Human Nutrition	Professor C.G. King, President, International Union of Nutritional Sciences, St Luke's Hospital Center, Amsterdam Avenue at 114th Street, New York, New York 10025, U.S.A.
Socio-demographic and Population Dynamics Studies	Dr J. Sutter, Institut National d'Etudes Demographiques, 23—25 Avenue Franklin D. Roosevelt, Paris, VIIIᵉ, France
Studies of Migrant and Isolate Groups	Professor F.S. Hulse, Department of Anthropology, University of Arizona, Tucson, Arizona 85721, U.S.A.

B IMPLEMENTATION

1 NATIONAL LEVEL

a National programmes

It is the responsibility of national committees to formulate their programme in the light of the resources, funds and personnel available to them, and of course, the prevailing interests and international research connections of workers in human biology. Specifically, national contributions should be presented for Phase I and II, and the detailed items to be considered are specified in this guide. It is of paramount importance that national committees and correspondents furnish the information requested in as full detail as possible. To reiterate briefly, national contributions are composed of the following:

For Phase I—1964–67:

a   Helping to formulate recommended agreed methods.
b   Helping with research on methodology.
c   Taking part in training schemes.
d   Undertaking pilot investigations.

For Phase II—1967–72:

Choosing the research topics in conformity with the categories described and explained above, indicating areas and communities of interest.

Following receipt of the information, comments on national contributions and suggestions for co-operation with other countries, etc., will be made to the different nations by the Sectional Committee.

b Research direction and finance

The detailed formulation for research and its execution will be the responsibility of the national research committee and the team concerned. They will also undertake co-ordinated planning discussions with those countries with whom co-operation in a particular region or topic is desirable. National teams will be free to call on the 'central' bodies or bureaux of the IBP and any of the U.N. agencies involved (it is hoped, in particular, WHO).

Nearly every research topic listed in the programme in sections II and III is envisaged as requiring three stages of study.

1   *A preliminary stage* in which the extent of the problem will be defined by reference to existing knowledge and in which arrangements (financial,

personnel, technical, etc.) will be made for carrying out the next stage, the pilot study.

2 *Pilot study*. This will be concerned mainly with obtaining preliminary information in the field and making possible the organization necessary for stage 3.

3 *Full scale study*. This would last for two years or more and would be *phased* according to the emphasis given. For example, the genetics study might be followed or preceded by physiological, medical or other studies.

The cost of national or multi-national projects will be borne by the countries concerned, as was the case in the International Geophysical Year. Regional arrangements should certainly make possible the participation of many less well endowed countries by pooling of resources.

The plan for field research is, in the final resort, the responsibility of the teams concerned, in deciding the specific aims, design, sampling methods, hypotheses to be tested, etc. It will be obligatory for teams to use a minimum number of research methods as given in the IBP handbook(s), (they would be free to use additional and alternative methods as well).

c Submission of data

A standardized pro-forma for use in the field by research teams will be agreed upon and will be obligatory in order that the minimum data can be tabulated and processed using a punch card or tape recording system. On the IGY pattern it will be incumbent on participating countries to send basic observations on the agreed proforma to central data collection and tabulating centres. Teams will be free to publish the results in their own way, but the basic data will be tabulated to be available for future investigators.

d Ethical considerations

It is to be noted that, in dealing with communities in the field, research teams will be under special obligations to maintain a high ethical approach to the local populations.

2 INTERNATIONAL LEVEL

a Collation of national programmes

It will be the duty of the HA Sectional Committee to collate and comment constructively on all the various national programmes and to offer such help to nations as can be made available through the Convener, the consultants and advisers, W.H.O. and the office of SCIBP. To this end a register of all projects is to be compiled.

b For Phase I

i The compilation of a methodology handbook is a major responsibility of the Convener.

ii The Sectional Committee, the Convener and the Consultants will endeavour to organise the promotion of training schemes by drawing up lists of laboratories willing to give training and by helping to arrange interchange of students.

c For Phase II

The major concern of the Sectional Committee, the Convener and SCIBP, will be

i To facilitate international co-operation in the launching of particular field projects;

ii to establish 'consultant' services;

iii to establish one or more data centres for storage and retrieval of data, and also as a documentation centre;

iv to organise conferences and symposia to survey results obtained.

Appendix

Multidisciplinary Studies of Human Adaptability; Theoretical Justification and Method

PAUL T. BAKER
Department of Anthropology
The Pennsylvania State University

Man, in his process of evolution, has become the most widespread terrestrial animal in the entire spectrum of chordates. He has also created the most complex social environment of all the animals. These two well accepted facts delineate the complexity of the task ahead when we endeavour to understand human adaptability. Clearly, no animal has adapted to a broader range of physical environment nor has any other animal created such a wide diversity of environments by his own endeavours. It is perhaps this culture creating capacity of man that has often confounded efforts to study human adaptability in the past. It has also led many biologists into adopting the attitude that the study of human adaptability lies almost entirely within the province of the social scientists. Even such a great biologist as Darwin, in attempting to explain the evolution of man, finally concluded that the cultural factors must be evoked as a primary explanation for the biological existence and diversity of man. However, in recent years evidence has indicated that, in spite of culture, man can be studied as an animal and that in the process of his evolution man had to adapt to the same environmental stresses as did his relatives in the animal kingdom.

A re-examination of evolution from a theoretical viewpoint and an examination of the factual data has shown that man, as other mammals, has been subject to the selective pressures of the physical and biological environment and has responded not only by the process of culture formation but also by the process of biological adaptation. We may, therefore, probably investigate human adaptability by beginning with the concepts of the ecologists, first examining man's relationship to the biological environment but also remembering that he has created a new category of environment—the cultural environment. Culture remains the most elusive element since it not only creates adaptations to the previous environment but also creates stresses within itself to which man must adapt as surely as he must adapt to the physical world.

Of equal significance to the problem of studying human adaptability is the enormous variety of adaptational mechanisms which man has available. He, as all other animals, may adapt to a new form of environmental stress by mutational change and by subsequent changes in gene frequency. Indeed, as recent studies have shown, this has probably been more common than had been assumed. However, the enormous range of adaptive mechanisms which man has available are primarily the consequence of the rising somatic and behavioral plasticity which seems to have occurred through the mammalian evolutionary process, culminating at the moment, in man.

One of the secular trends in mammalian evolution was the rise in phenotypic plasticity which increasingly allowed animals to vary their pattern of functioning and behavior in response to the information provided by the environment in which they developed. Man's culture creating capacity might be considered the inevitable end product of this increasing plasticity. The most apparent aspect of increasing plasticity was the increasing ability to learn.

The most important single attribute for the development of culture is man's enormous learning capacity; which in biological terms might simply be referred to as his high ability to pattern his behavior in response to the environmental challenges. Of equal consequence to studies of human adaptability is man's functional and morphological plasticity. The functional and morphological plasticity of man is probably most familiar to us in its short term manifestations. For example, temperature and altitude acclimatization are well documented examples of modification in the functioning of man which increase his performance capability in the face of new environmental stress. Other examples would be the increase in muscle fibre size which accompanies exercise or the psychological process of accustomization which allows the organism to ignore distracting stimuli in the environment. Perhaps equally important, but less well studied, are the long term adaptive changes which occur in human beings when they develop under particular types of environmental stress. For example, children, when they must exist in a caloric deficient environment can do so for prolonged periods of time by a cessation of growth which, if the deprivation period is not of excessive length, will later be recouped. In the same vein, man has the capacity to store calories in the form of fat when he has available 'more than adequate' calories. These stored calories can later be used during periods of short calorie supply. Other examples which can be cited include the increased size of the lungs and the heart which occur in individuals who grow up in a high altitude environment with its low oxygen pressure.

Less is known of the possibilities of long term improvements in physiological function but possible examples include the increased tolerance of drugs over long exposure.

Thus, if we take a broad view of the problem of studying human adaptability we see that man has such a large variety of environmental stresses to which he adapts and such a large variety of mechanisms available to him for adaptation that we are probably dealing with a fairly unique set of interactions in each human population that is studied. More than with any other animal, we must take great care to identify properly the stresses to which a human population has been exposed and to consider all of the parameters of adaptation man has available to solve the problem of survival in a given environment.

METHODOLOGICAL PROBLEMS IN THE STUDY OF HUMAN ADAPTABILITY

1 Identifying primary stresses

The uniqueness of the environmental stress pattern for each human population presents some particular problems in the methodology of studying human adaptation. Primary among these problems is the identification of the stresses within the environment of a given group. Although simple indices such as mean annual temperature or the crude birth rate are suggestive of environmental stress, the flexibility of human adaptation makes them unsuitable as *prima facie* evidence of an environmental stress. Among the most straightforward methods of determining the stresses to which a population is exposed is a catalogue of the causes of death and sterility. However, this also may be misleading, since where reported, the causes of death are always recorded as the most immediate causes and tell virtually nothing of the predisposing factors which may be the underlying causes of death. Furthermore, both cause of death and sterility data are almost totally unavailable for the majority of peasant and primitive populations which must be a primary concern of our studies.

The second method of determining the significant environmental stresses is an evaluation of the stresses which would severely strain the human homeostatic processes. I have emphasized the words *severe strain* because it is of little value to consider those stresses which place only a modest strain upon homeostatic processes. A modest strain may be equated with stimulation and as such is a necessity since lack of stimulation leads to atrophy.

The methodological difficulties of identifying these primary stresses within human populations leads at this point in time to the selection of stress situations which are obvious; with a deferment to a later point in time, a consideration of the more subtle stresses. For example, in considering the stresses imposed by the physical environment, it is quite obvious that in human populations who live above 4000 meters the organism is encountering a severe strain caused by a reduced oxygen tension. This can be measured by the massive changes that occur both during development and short term exposure. It is equally apparent that when we measure a micro-environment of man and find his nude skin exposed to temperatures below 15° centigrade or above 30° centigrade, the homeostatic mechanisms are not easily compensating for the temperature load which is being imposed.

There are also biological environment stresses. For example, situations in which protein content is extremely low in the diet produce pathologies in human development such as kwashiorkor, or a diet with an excessive niacin deficiency will result in pellagra. Malaria and intestinal parasites form major stresses for large segments of the human population both now and for a considerable measure of time in the past. In terms of cultural environment stress, it is more difficult to identify even the primary stresses, but cultural constructs which specify sexual access patterns are highly significant in determining the trends of gene changes which have elicited adaptation. It has been suggested recently that man, as other animals, may be subjected to rather severe stress in the presence of crowding.

Of these highly evident forms of stress to which man has adapted, the most easily quantified and the most consistent through time are the stresses imposed by the physical and biological environment. This is in no sense an effort to underrate the importance of the stresses which have been introduced by the cultural environment, but those produced by the cultural environment have changed rapidly. Furthermore, many are of such recent origin that we may often limit our consideration of the responses to the plastic responses of man and exclude genetic adaptation.

2 Determining the degree of adaptation in human populations

Turning for the moment from the question of identifying the stresses in the environment, we may ask how successful adaptation can be measured in a human population. Perhaps the most correct measure provided by evolutionary theory is survival; not necessarily survival of the individual but rather survival of the group and the members of that group. If a group has survived in a given environment for a period of many generations it may be considered adapted even though some members remain maladapted. However, this does not mean that a new group will not displace it in the near future because of a more successful set of adaptations. By the same measure when a population of human beings is placed in a new environment, a rising number of individuals is indicative of a high degree of adaptation while declining numbers indicate a lack of success in adaptation. Of course, instability in population numbers, whether growth or loss, basically represents an unstable ecological situation for man as for any other animal, and it may be exceedingly difficult to evaluate the significance of these changes until stability has occurred. Our inability to define accurately adaptation in unstable populations is one of the best arguments in favor of the study of primitive and peasant populations where stability has occurred and where we may, therefore, hope to define more carefully the mechanisms which have permitted this stable adaptation in the population.

Another measure of the degree of success of adaptation in human populations can be derived from an accurate assessment of the human micro-environment. A careful assessment of the micro-environment, which is here defined as the significant environment for the functioning of man's homeostatic systems, provides us with the significant measure of the cultural adaptive system. This system includes all the non-biological components which protect man from the natural environment. By contrasting the natural environment with the micro-environment we may assess the degree to which man's culture has modified his natural environment in directions which reduce the stress on his biological system.

The Eskimo culture has often been cited as an example of a complex of cultural traits which are so successful in protecting the group from the external, natural conditions that the micro-environment of the Eskimo supposedly contains very little cold stress. This may be true, but our final measure of the validity of this statement must rest on a careful assessment of the total micro-temperature environment of the Eskimo during his normal life cycle.

To cite but one more example, it has often been stressed by anthropologists that groups do not utilize all the food resources found in their natural environment and that, therefore, no true picture of the nutritional characteristics of a group can be obtained by a description of the food found in the natural environment. By the same token, individual variation in nutritional patterns is so great that even a definition of the food stuffs available within a household is not an adequate picture of the nutritional intakes of the various members of the households.

While the assessment of the micro-environment permits us to evaluate the degree of cultural adaptation for a given population, it is only by a direct comparison of the functional capacity of two populations within one stress situation that we learn the degree of physiological tolerance of a population to the stress. It is to be hoped that at some time in the future we will understand the adaptive mechanisms of man with sufficient clarity so that measurements of physiological response to stress made on one population may be compared with other studies made under different conditions. However, at present the only method which provides us with any certainty in our conclusion is the one of direct comparison of two or more groups under identical conditions.

In summary then, if we wish to determine the degree of adaptation to a given set of environmental stress for a human population: (1) we must determine the nature and determinants of the demographic structure of that population; (2) we must determine the micro-environment in which the group operates; and (3) we must determine the degree of its functional capability in the presence of the stress by a direct comparison with other human groups exposed to comparable conditions.

3 Determining the sources of adaptation

The methods outlined in the previous discussion permit a rough differentiation between the cultural methods of adaptation and the biological methods of adaptation, but it tells us nothing of the sources of these adaptations. If we consider first cultural adaptations, we may define their degree of success by the extent to which the natural environment has been modified to suit man's needs. However, a partition of the cultural components and the determination of their ultimate source is an exceedingly difficult task. I will not in this paper attempt to outline methods in this task with any detail. However, it might be pointed out that cultural adaptations can be conveniently divided into material culture items with which men modify the environment in contrast to behavioral patterns which modify exposure.

While the sources of cultural adaptation to stresses remain obscure in the problems of understanding human learning and culture transmission, the sources of biological adaptation can be conceived even though we still do not have available all of the methods required to partition the biological components of adaptation precisely. As was noted earlier in the paper, the sources of biological adaptation may be categorized into four types. These are: psychological accommodation, physiological acclimatization, developmental acclimatization or adaptation, and genetic adaptation.

The study of these sources requires different methodologies. Psychological accommodation may be investigated in the laboratory situation with great profit. For example, evidence has accumulated in recent years that much of the peripheral temperature hunting response, which has been noted in groups such as Eskimo and fishermen, may be related to central nervous system accommodation. A great deal may be learned by extensive laboratory studies of this phenomenon. Short term acclimatization may also be studied fruitfully in the laboratory situation. However, problems of determining developmental acclimatization and genetic adaptation will require a much more elaborate methodology involving us in the study of populations in the field as well as in the laboratory.

We have now reached a state of knowledge where we can state that there are differences in the biological adaptation of human populations to particular types of stresses such as climate and altitude. It will, therefore, be our most pressing task in the next few years to try to define the sources of these differences and categorize them within the above classification.

METHODOLOGICAL SOLUTIONS WHICH CAN BE APPLIED TO FIELD SITUATIONS

Having considered some of the broad methodological problems involved in the study of human adaptability, it becomes obvious that no single discipline has sufficient techniques or conceptual frameworks with which to study all the aspects of human adaptation. Indeed, each discipline is, within our present academic and scientific structure, capable of contributing to only limited parts of the total problem. A multiple disciplinary attack upon the problem, limited to a selected group of populations which exists under obvious environmental stress situations, will provide us with more information and more insights than a series of disconnected studies concerned with only single aspects of the overall problem.

Given such a goal a method or methods must be developed which allows each discipline to bring to bear its own particular abilities yet retains organization within the population studies. At least two alternatives may be suggested. The first might be termed the epidemiological or shotgun approach. Within this method, a community would be selected and all of the data which were conceivably pertinent to adaptation would be collected on the population. This would contain the broad spectrum of information which has generally been outlined under the proposed IBP study of human adaptability and would include such things as demographic characteristics, genetic polymorphisms, health, heat and cold tolerance, disease patterns, nutrition, etc. Once these data were compiled, extensive inter-correlations could be made to determine the degree of association between the various findings.

Other authors have discussed the virtues of this basic method, but in this paper I would like to develop an alternative method which has a more focalized goal and is, therefore, capable of generating more specific data on adaptation.

If the alternative and complementary nature of biological and cultural adaptation is explored, several imperatives may be derived which provide useful guides for human adaptation research.

1. Adaptations occur as responses to selective stresses. These stresses may be divided into those which arise from two sources, even though both are found in all societies.

(a) Those derived from being a human animal in any environment, e.g., need to reproduce, eat, sleep, etc. These give rise to what may be called cultural and bio-adaptational universals.

(b) Those derived from the fact that different environments have produced different stresses so that variation in adaptation is a necessary aspect of any variation in the environment. Thus, the variations in the physical environment, biotic environment or pre-existent culture produce different adaptations for specific group survival.

2. Since man has available both cultural and biological methods of adaptation, there appears very little logical justification for assuming that only one of these modes of response will be encountered in a group's adaptation to a given stress. Technological invention, as an adaptive response to stress, has the obvious advantage of more rapid transmission than is possible in genetic adaptation. The rapid development and dissemination of a new vaccine in response to a new flu virus in western society suggests that culture is a more flexible and rapid method than gene change for adapting man to his environmental stresses. This appears to be a valid generalization, yet in more stable societies the cultural response has seldom been so rapid or successful. The detailed studies of malaria have uncovered not only a plethora of cultural adaptations to this disease but also a wide variety of genetic adaptations, a combination of which seems necessary for group survival. Therefore, it seems that in investigating adaptation to any form of selective stress, the *a priori* hypothesis should be that both cultural and biological adaptation will be present.

The previous deductions, based on the assumption that variation in man's culture and biology is adaptive, open a broad research possibility for understanding variation in those human attributes. One needs only to find for a given society a stress which will produce severe strain and the group may then be studied in terms of the modes of adaptation. Such a study does not have to be concerned with the attitudes or values which the population manifests in relation to the trait. It must be assumed that most cultural as well as biological traits serve multiple functions. If one wishes to understand the total pattern by which a population is adjusted to a given stress, then the adaptive utility of a trait to that given stress is the only aspect which need be studied. This generality is equally valid for both cultural and biological traits. Thus, if a study is made of how Quechua Indians have adapted to the mammalian need for calcium, it may be stated that the practice of chewing coca with *cal* (a substance containing more than 40% usable calcium) helps the population adapt to this need.

It is of no consequence to this particular study that the population values the coca chewing as a method of alleviating discomfort nor is it significant that the social scientist observes that coca chewing provides status and group identification for the individual. Of course, the manifest and latent social function of the traits may have adaptive value to other forms of cultural stress the same as calcium ingestion is probably not the only biological consequence of this behavior. However, this point has been emphasized in order to show how the study of biological and cultural adaptation may be reduced to a manageable methodology. It will probably never be possible to know all of the adaptive functions served by the simplest of cultural or biological traits in a human community, but by the systematic study of the total biological and cultural adaptive pattern in relation to a single environment stress, we may hope gradually to accumulate sufficient data so that we may understand how these components work together to guarantee the survival of a human community.

Once information has been collected on the total adaptational pattern of a human community to a single stress, we have open two alternative paths for continued research. We may study another human community in relation to its adaptation to the same kind of stress. For example, we might compare the adaptational pattern to cold between Eskimos and Chuckchis. Alternatively, we may pick another stress within the same community and define its adaptational pattern with the intention of then relating the two adaptational patterns. In either instance the study requires more than a single discipline. For example, even in the comparison of cold tolerance, several disciplines should be represented. A minimum study would call for the competencies of anthropologists, both cultural and physical, environmental physiologists plus guidance by a statistician on sampling and analysis.

The second basic design which calls for studying adaptation to multiple stresses in a single group would demand an even broader representation. It appears at this time that the latter design promises a greater return for the effort since it will allow the study of such complex problems as the interaction between cold tolerance, nutrition, body structure and physical fitness. At the same time, the second approach, since it involves so many disciplines, presents the complex problems associated with the mechanics of a broad based multidisciplinary study.

MECHANICS OF A MULTIDISCIPLINARY STUDY

It is probably not an exaggeration to say that the majority of multidisciplinary studies have failed in their full purpose. On the positive side, they have reduced research costs by permitting a group of scientists to use the same facilities and test subjects. However, most often the results obtained on different aspects of the problem are never integrated. The reason for these failures of integration are diverse but appear often to stem from the lack of a firm structure and the subsequent fact that the members of one discipline do not trust the ability of other discipline members to interpret their data. Other problems include publication privileges and the failure of some investigators to prepare their results.

Some of these problems may be solved by careful planning at the beginning of a study but no amount of planning can prevent the occasional breakdown of multidisciplinary studies. To reduce these breakdowns, at least two alternative structures may be established.

1. A senior person with some competence in all the subject areas may be in charge with the clear understanding that he has full authority over the conduct of the project and has publication rights to all data.

2. The project may have an administrative director who is also a scientist and a group of individual discipline scientists who have control of their individual studies. In this structure it is imperative that all data be available to each investigator. Publication priorities and schedules must be carefully established in advance.

Neither of these systems is fully satisfactory. The first contains all the hazards which arise from depending on a single person while the second one, no matter how carefully structured, often ends without any integration of the results. No structure can do away with the need for mutual respect among the scientists involved in a study. However, structure is essential because the most compatible men in a university atmosphere may develop a strong dislike for each other in a field situation which is often uncomfortable.

The proper procedural organization for a multidisciplinary field study can not only reduce friction but also greatly increase efficiency. If it is assumed that most of the larger multidisciplinary field studies will be done on primitive or simple peasant cultures then certain procedural guide lines may be developed.

(1) Pick a major emphasis for the study—as stated earlier it is better to choose an easily identifiable stress which has already been demonstrated to severely stress non-adapted people.

(2) Conduct a pilot study on the population to be investigated. The pilot study should provide good sample information on the demography, general life cycle, physical environment and micro-environment. Depending on the size of the population, these data can usually be collected by one professional with one or more technical assistants over a period of one year.

(3) The data from the pilot study will provide, upon analysis, the following information necessary for the proper conduct of the major study.

(a) General information on the extent to which the culture is modifying the apparent stress.

(b) The nature of other stresses in the environment not superficially evident.

(c) The number of people available for different types of research designs.

(d) The best time of the year for various types of studies.

(e) In the case of small primitive cultures it may be important to determine the nature of the general culture before the larger research group modifies the structure.

(4) Of prime importance in the next step towards the major study is the provision of a field laboratory. In most large studies some form of laboratory is required. Because of varying discipline requirements, no set guide can be given on the nature of this laboratory.

In some instances semi-permanent buildings may be called for while in other studies various forms of portable laboratories may be best suited. For studies involving small populations the transporting of small groups to existent facilities should always be considered.

(5) Beyond this step, planning will vary considerably depending on the principal emphasis, but it is probably worthwhile to point out a few of the hazards and potential safeguards.

(a) Always allow more time than appears necessary and more technicians than essential. Work in new areas produces unexpected delays and investigators usually contract a variety of minor diseases which reduce efficiency.

(b) Plan intensive studies in blocks of time which do not exceed a month without a brief vacation. There can, of course, be exceptions to this but when a group of several individuals must work closely together, minor frictions can develop into major ones if occasional breaks are not provided.

(c) The general development of the human adaptability programme will be better served and the total data collection will be greater if advanced graduate students are heavily utilized in the multidisciplinary studies. While these students will often need some supervision this can usually be accomplished by one or two professionals working with students from a variety of disciplines.

(d) Finally there will always be difficulties arising from working with human test subjects. These are likely to be more severe with the multidisciplinary studies because the variety of demands placed on the subject population and the longer study period allows more time for the development of rumors and animosities. It is, therefore, essential that close contact with the subject population be maintained through an anthropologist. Different cultures will have different taboos and fears. These can be violated but the price and consequences will necessarily be high. In general primitive and peasant populations are no more difficult to work with than civilized ones and the attractive power of money and material goods is still the best inducement for test subjects.

INTEGRATION OF THE MULTIDISCIPLINARY STUDY INTO HA-IBP GOALS

The human adaptability project of the IBP has generally been designed so as to allow an understanding of the variability in human adaptability by the comparative technique. Thus by the comparison of the physical growth or physical fitness of a variety of peoples throughout the world we hope to understand the extent of variability and something of the mechanisms which produce variability in development and fitness. In the present report, a structure has been developed which emphasizes the study of single human populations. It, therefore, should be pointed out that the utility of these studies will ultimately rest on the comparative approach. A measure of the micro-environment of cold or activity structure for a human population means little unless we have comparable data for other human groups.

Of equal importance, the large scale multidisciplinary studies will provide the necessary background for the interpretation of the single phase studies such as simple physical growth measurements. Thus it is apparent that a carefully planned series of large scale multidisciplinary studies which draws on the diverse talents of the scientists from many countries will form an important aspect of the overall program for the study of Human Adaptability.